Currere and Psychoanalytic Guided Regression

This book revisits the 1970 Kent State shootings, also known as the May 4 massacre and the Kent State massacre, using a new approach of *currere* and psychoanalytic guided regression. Drawing on a variety of interviews with those who were present at the events or who have close connections to the aftermath, the author engages in what he terms a doubled *currere*. This includes weaving a description of *currere* and narrative work with the actual storytelling of the subjects in order to build bridges and positive meaning through allegory and through inquiry that honors the narrative and re-energizes the field. Using a combination of the interviews, analysis and synthesis, the book re-activates and re-vitalizes the events, crucially engages with the notion of alterity, and unpacks the singularity of the past in its distinctive complexity. Carrying themes of hopeful ambiguity, it demonstrates how positive change can be guided, and positive insights engendered. Constructing a new remembrance of these tragic events and offering a distinctive and unique study utilizing *currere*, it will appeal to scholars of curriculum and instruction, as well as psychiatrists, psychologists, and historians.

Karl Martin is Adjunct Instructor at Kent State University, USA.

Studies in Curriculum Theory Series
Series Editor: William F. Pinar,
University of British Columbia, Canada

In this age of multimedia information overload, scholars and students may not be able to keep up with the proliferation of different topical, trendy book series in the field of curriculum theory. It will be a relief to know that one publisher offers a balanced, solid, forward-looking series devoted to significant and enduring scholarship, as opposed to a narrow range of topics or a single approach or point of view. This series is conceived as the series busy scholars and students can trust and depend on to deliver important scholarship in the various "discourses" that comprise the increasingly complex field of curriculum theory.

The range of the series is both broad (all of curriculum theory) and limited (only important, lasting scholarship) – including but not confined to historical, philosophical, critical, multicultural, feminist, comparative, international, aesthetic, and spiritual topics and approaches. Books in this series are intended for scholars and for students at the doctoral and, in some cases, master's levels.

Women Curriculum Theorists
Power, Knowledge and Subjectivity
Sandra Leaton Gray and David Scott

Love in the Post-Reconceptualist Era of Curriculum Work
Deliberations on the Meanings of Care
Allan Michel Jales Coutinho

South Korean Education and Learning Excellence as a Hallyu
Ethnographic Understandings of a Nation's Academic Success
Young Chun Kim, Jae-seong Jo, and Jung-Hoon Jung

Currere and Psychoanalytic Guided Regression
Revisiting the Kent State Shootings
Karl Martin

For more information about this series, please visit: https://www.routledge.com/Studies-in-Curriculum-Theory-Series/book-series/LEASCTS

Currere and Psychoanalytic Guided Regression
Revisiting the Kent State Shootings

Karl Martin

NEW YORK AND LONDON

First published 2024
by Routledge
605 Third Avenue, New York, NY 10158

and by Routledge
4 Park Square, Milton Park, Abingdon, Oxon, OX14 4RN

Routledge is an imprint of the Taylor & Francis Group, an informa business

© 2024 Karl Martin

The right of Karl Martin to be identified as author of this work has been asserted in accordance with sections 77 and 78 of the Copyright, Designs and Patents Act 1988.

All rights reserved. No part of this book may be reprinted or reproduced or utilised in any form or by any electronic, mechanical, or other means, now known or hereafter invented, including photocopying and recording, or in any information storage or retrieval system, without permission in writing from the publishers.

Trademark notice: Product or corporate names may be trademarks or registered trademarks, and are used only for identification and explanation without intent to infringe.

Library of Congress Cataloging-in-Publication Data
Names: Martin, Karl W., 1951- author.
Title: Currere and psychoanalytic guided regression : revisiting the Kent State shootings / Karl Martin.
Description: New York, NY : Routledge, 2024. | Series: Studies in curriculum theory | Includes bibliographical references and index.
Identifiers: LCCN 2023010844 (print) | LCCN 2023010845 (ebook) | ISBN 9781032503479 (hardback) | ISBN 9781032505718 (paperback) | ISBN 9781003399094 (ebook)
Subjects: LCSH: Kent State Shootings, Kent, Ohio, 1970--Psychological aspects. | Kent State Shootings, Kent, Ohio, 1970--Biography. | Regression analysis. | Episodic memory.
Classification: LCC LD4191.O72 M37 2024 (print) | LCC LD4191.O72 (ebook) | DDC 973.924--dc23/eng/20230426
LC record available at https://lccn.loc.gov/2023010844
LC ebook record available at https://lccn.loc.gov/2023010845

ISBN: 978-1-032-50347-9 (hbk)
ISBN: 978-1-032-50571-8 (pbk)
ISBN: 978-1-003-39909-4 (ebk)

DOI: 10.4324/9781003399094

Typeset in Times New Roman
by SPi Technologies India Pvt Ltd (Straive)

Dedicated to Allison Krause, Jeffrey Miller, Sandra Scheuer and William Schroeder…and to those who survived.

Contents

About the Author — ix
Acknowledgments — x

1 Currere and Psychoanalytic Guided Regression: Revisiting the Kent State Shootings — 1

2 History and Currere — 9

3 Sophie Freud — 31

4 Patricia Gless — 41

5 Jerry M. Lewis, Professor Emeritus — 43

6 Alan Canfora, Lifelong Activist — 49

7 Lynn Csernotta Beaton, Artist and Teacher — 56

8 Nancy Csernotta Joyce — 64

9 John Cleary, Architect — 71

10 Joe Cullum — 82

11 Roseann "Chic" Canfora — 97

12 The 1970s and My Journey of Understanding — 105

13	Representative Patricia Morgan	112
14	The Music: Jason Hanley	115
15	Final Notes	120
	Index	*132*

About the Author

Karl Martin PhD is Adjunct Instructor at Kent State University, USA. An experienced teacher with a demonstrated history of working in the higher education industry, he is skilled in educational technology, student development, social media, adult education, writing, art, and music. His higher education classes place a focus on developing and refining teacher identity and application of Deweyan problem-solving within a democratic society. Students are encouraged to apply these skills to their own practice, whether this is concerned with art education, studio art, or middle-childhood inquiry.

Acknowledgments

Sincere thanks to Dr. William Pinar, for believing in me.
    and to my colleagues James G. Henderson, Jennifer Schneider, Jennifer Lowers, Tom Poetter, John J. Stuhr, Frank X. Ryan, Rick Newton, Sheryl Chatfield, Olga Umansky and Martha Watson. I am especially grateful for their support and stimulus:

to editor Alice Salt, who has shepherded me through the manuscript. There is no better.

to editor Sophie Ganesh, for her sage counsel,
    and to Lauren Redhead for her expertise.

My immense gratitude to those who have shared their stories: Lynn Csernotta Beaton, Alan Canfora, Roseann Canfora, John Cleary, Joe Cullum, Sophie Freud, Patricia Gless, Nancy Csernotta Joyce, Jerry M. Lewis, Patricia Morgan, and Pamela Vanags.

Thank you to Elizabeth Campion, Cynthia Kristof, Anita Clary, Kathleen Medicus,
    and all the professionals at the Kent State University Library and Archives.

Thanks to Jason Hanley, from the *Rock and Roll Hall of Fame*,
    and to the Kent Historical Society.

Special thanks to photographers John Darnell, Paul Gailey, William Cogliano and John Filo.

and to the coffee emporium folk. You know who you are.

Above all, I owe my deepest gratitude to my wife Michelle and my family.

1 Currere and Psychoanalytic Guided Regression
Revisiting the Kent State Shootings

Introduction

I was 60 miles away, finishing up freshman year at Westminster, a small liberal arts college. It was a Monday – 20 minutes until dinner, two weeks until finals, and three years until graduation. Westminster College had the same sunny, cool start to a spring week as Kent State. After a long day of classes, students returned to Russell Hall, serving as both dorm and cafeteria. A dog named Aristotle wandered about near a large Sylvania television set. We watched daily updates about faraway places like Da Nang and Hanoi, taking note of battlefield casualties.

Walter Cronkite's somber face appeared, and someone turned up the volume. What we saw was chilling, stupefying. Four students had been killed and nine wounded at Kent State University while protesting President Richard M. Nixon's decision to invade Cambodia. The sight of military units on a college campus was infuriating. Only a handful of zealots were sympathetic to the Vietnam War. College men had "II-S" deferments, excused from the military for scholarship.

My experience with the Selective Service System began a year earlier, on my 18th birthday. We weren't allowed to vote, but all men of that age had to register. After I completed the required forms, a World War II veteran from the draft board offered his opinion: "I hope you flunk out so that we can ship your sorry ass to Vietnam." The II S deferment saved a lot of us from serving in what we saw as an unjust war. Nobody – *nobody* – believed the prevailing anti-communist rhetoric. Even world champion boxer Muhammed Ali weighed in, telling reporters in Louisville that he would refuse induction: "I ain't got no quarrel with those Vietcong. Why should they ask me to put on a uniform and go 10,000 miles from home and drop bombs and bullets on brown people in Vietnam after so-called Negro people in Louisville are treated like dogs and denied simple human rights?" (Orkland, 2017). An all-white Texas jury convicted Ali for draft evasion, and he went to prison. The verdict was later overturned by the Supreme Court.

DOI: 10.4324/9781003399094-1

2 Currere and Psychoanalytic Guided Regression

Based on an individual registrant's circumstances and beliefs, draft eligibility determined who was deferred, exempted, or available for military service. Stated another way, a young man's educational experiences were tied in with his draft eligibility. If your family could afford to send you to college, deferments were applied for higher education. Biased in that it favored those with the money to spend on college, poor Whites, Blacks, and Latinos were often conscripted into the military. My last draft card was issued just prior to my student teaching experience in Ellwood City, Pennsylvania.

1-H was a "good" classification, meaning that one wasn't scheduled for military service.

The 1-A classification meant eight weeks of basic training, a trip to Vietnam, and a possible death sentence. I was lucky because the draft ended when I completed my BA in art education. In 1973, I began graduate study in the Department of Education as a teaching assistant. After earning my master's degree, I was offered a job teaching visual art for Kent City Schools.

Kent State University

Given the prevailing sentiments against the escalation of the Vietnam War, it's easy to visualize and understand the reactions to President Nixon's address to the nation on Thursday, April 30, 1970. He had begun a process called "Vietnamization," announced on November 3, 1969 (during my senior year of high school) providing for a gradual withdrawal of American troops. Contrary to his promises, Nixon secretly began bombing campaigns in Cambodia, considered a neutral nation. This incursion into Cambodia did come to public attention, and he was harshly criticized. This prompted anti-war demonstrations across America, and anti-war activism surfaced as demonstrations at Kent State University.

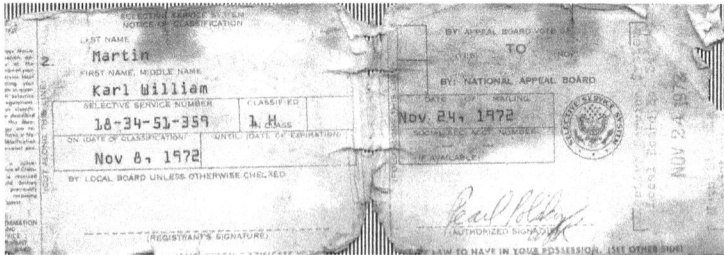

Figure 1.1 Selective Service Registration, known colloquially as a "Draft Card". Karl Martin, 1972. At age 18, young men were required to register with their local draft boards and were required to always carry their draft cards with them. The *Draft Card Mutilation Act* of 1965 made it a criminal offense to burn a draft card.

When I moved to Kent four years later, I was astonished by the reactionary views of the community. Even former Kent State University president Robert White had been surprised when the residents of Kent showed deep hostility toward the university: "[T]here is little criticism of the Guard and the belief is frequently expressed that they should have shot more of them" (Kifner, 1970, p. 23). Patriotic townspeople thought that printing the high school photos of the victims was wrong because they "were dirty and they had long hair" (p. 23). Kent Mayor LeRoy Satrom and his henchmen disavowed beatings of "hippie types" after the shootings and felt that any further disturbances should be addressed by police and guardsmen with loaded weapons.

The consequences of the Kent State shootings point to human shortsightedness. It is risky to assume that because people hold positions of responsibility they will therefore act accordingly. The five days leading up to the shootings and the horror of the event itself and the aftermath are well-documented. The proximity of the shootings to Taylor Hall and the school of journalism allowed for the accurate documentation of a massacre by forces representing law and order. The outcome would have been much worse if Glenn Frank hadn't been able to convince the seated 200 students to leave. Brigadier General Robert Canterbury and the guard were ready to advance again, and orders were given to shoot if the demonstrators didn't disperse.

Spring semester ended at Westminster College, and I returned home to Baltimore, family, and summer employment pumping gas and lifeguarding. Kent State was always in the back of our minds as we argued endlessly with parents and authority figures. Washington, DC, was nearby, and anti-war protestors were perpetually outside the Capital Building and the White House. Life had changed for us. We had become disillusioned, cynical. As new information came to light, we realized we were right. A few years later, the Pentagon Papers were leaked by Daniel Ellsberg, confirming what we knew all along: The escalation of the Vietnam War was based on an accumulation of lies from high-ranking government officials, including Presidents Johnson and Nixon. The shooting of unarmed students on their own campus began the end of the Vietnam era, and I wanted to find out more from persons who were *there*, on-site – during the events that led up to and including the shootings.

This represents a new approach to the events and tragedy of May 4, 1970, at Kent State University using the Method of Currere. I will forward a psychoanalytic technique that encourages curriculum stakeholders to consider and undertake the four phases of currere. This is not psychoanalysis or therapy but rather a response to suggestions that participants "reactivate" their experiences. "Reactivation is, then, a reformulation of the regressive phase of *currere*, encouraging not only remembrance of things past, but also a return to their presence there, a temporal regression in service of reconstructing one's subjective experience of the present" (Pinar, 2017, p. 1).

4 *Currere and Psychoanalytic Guided Regression*

Figure 1.2 National Guard personnel walking toward crowd near Taylor Hall, tear gas has been fired (Ronald P. McNees. May 4 Collection. Kent State University Libraries. Special Collections and Archives).

To write about the shootings at Kent State University on May 4, 1970, is daunting. There have been many books, histories, essays, and memoirs written on the subject, but fewer and fewer as time goes on. As a college freshman at the time, I was keenly invested in *what* happened, *why* it happened, and *how* to interpret what happened. I wanted to know more, to understand those moments. Formal written and spoken statements abound, and events leading up to and including the shootings are easily accessed. I wanted to gather testimonies from people whom I'd met in educational settings. Their firsthand accounts and *currere* narratives offer new perspectives about that history.

Currere

The Method of Currere is an approach to education based on postmodern philosophy and psychoanalytic technique, first described in a 1975 paper by William Pinar. *Currere* is a four-step process: regressive – progressive – analytical – synthetical. The steps don't always have to be undertaken in a prescribed order, and a *Guided Currere Narrative* requires a regression into the autobiographical self and educational past, incorporating biography and historiography. I am interested in firsthand accounts of past and present educational experiences of persons who survived the shootings of May 4, 1970.

The aim is to provide a woven narrative tapestry composed of artifacts, material related to currere and education, and a mix of research and personal experience. The prevailing questions: How does this educational journey of researching the tragic events of that day and attempting to interpret their journeys affect my own? How does it offer a call to action to improve the world?

This research has enabled a few more pieces of the May 4 history to fit together. Uncovering *new* information is remote, but I encourage revisiting the stories of those who were on campus to engender new knowledge and insights:

> Insight comes, more often than not, from looking at what's been on the table all along, in front of everybody, rather than from discovering something new. Seeing is as much the job of an historian as it is of a poet or a painter, it seems to me. That's Dickens's great admonition to all writers, "Make me see."
>
> (McCullough et al., 1999, para 8)

I believe that the remembrances of those I've interviewed provide the reader with a look into those events from over half a century ago. They breathe life into May 4 with their regressions. My role is to encourage the participants to become part of the research through the method of currere. "The method reduces the distance between the researcher and subject by making the researcher the subject and allows for a deeper and clearer understanding of the present by outlining the past, present and future" (Pinar, 1975, p. 1). Whether or not this uncovers "truth" in the stories they share is interpretive. The reader may conduct an informal triangulation with what has been shared, identifying enough commonalities to establish what is conjecture and what is fact. We must be cautious with overgeneralizing, keeping in mind that there are beliefs at work, about how things were then and now, and hopeful predictions for the future. It's possible to do a small amount of testing and quantification. There are plenty of eyewitness accounts and photographic images to help with an empirical "scientism," but that isn't the intent here. Historians rely on storytelling, and the history of May 4 is no exception. People want – and deserve – to be allowed to tell their stories. It gives meaning to their experiences and ours.

What follows is a generalized description of how the events unfolded:

- On Thursday, April 30, 1970, the war escalated into Cambodia, with President Nixon reporting on national television that units would attack communist headquarters in Cambodia: "We shall avoid a wider war, but we are also determined to put an end to this war" (Orkland, 2017).

- Many student demonstrations erupted throughout the United States. At Kent State University, 500 students buried the Constitution, declaring that it had been murdered when troops were sent into Cambodia without a declaration of war by Congress.
- On Friday night the Water Street bars were packed, and some bottles were thrown at police cars.
- A fire was started on North Water Street. Windows were broken. Mayor Satrom imposed a midnight curfew, closed the bars, and ordered all the students back to the campus.
- More windows were broken, but some students helped the merchants clean up the damage on Saturday morning.
- The City of Kent fears a takeover. Mayor Leroy Satrom imposes an 8:00 p.m. curfew and calls for the Ohio National Guard.
- Dances are organized for Saturday night to mollify the angry students.
- The old ROTC building is burned. When the firemen arrive, some of their hoses are slashed. No police intervene (who, exactly, set the fire has never been established).
- Students try to go downtown to challenge the curfew, but units of the Ohio National Guard have arrived in Kent.
- The guard takes over the campus. Students are forced by bayonets back into their dormitories.
- Sunday morning, Governor James Rhodes arrives on campus, fanning the flames with alarmist rhetoric: "These people just move from one campus to the other and terrorize the community. They're worse than the brown shirts and the communist element than also the night riders and vigilantes are the worst type of people that we have in America."
- The Mayor of Kent states "We will take all necessary, I repeat all necessary actions to maintain law and order."
- On Sunday night, students sit down in the streets to block traffic, demanding that the guard leave the university. The university president is conveniently out of town.
- The guardsmen use bayonets and tear gas to force students back on campus.
- Helicopters hover overhead all night. There is resentment and fear.
- On Monday morning, Cambodia and Vietnam are secondary issues. The military occupation of a state university was primary.
- The students decide to hold a rally at noon.
- The guard and a university administrator pronounce it to be an illegal gathering. Students assemble at the victory bell.
- A jeep drives across the commons with a megaphone. Warnings are given to disperse.
- The Jeep Mission is unsuccessful, and General Canterbury orders the guardsmen to disperse the crowd.

- Troops advance with fixed bayonets, live ammunition, and tear gas. Students believe that freedom of speech and assembly are being denied.
- The students disperse, retreating up Blanket Hill. Allison Krause is spotted in photographs by the pagoda.
- Company C leaves, while the rest of the guard pursues students.
- The troops continue to march over Blanket Hill, turn left, and proceed downhill to a practice football field.
- A fence around the practice field impedes their march. Some rocks are thrown from the Prentice Hall parking lot.
- Tear gas canisters are thrown back and forth.
- Some of the guardsmen from Troop G huddle together by the practice field.
    They kneel and aim at Alan Canfora, who waves a black flag at them. (These troops were the first to fire.)
- An order is given to march back up Blanket Hill. Members of Troop G are photographed looking back toward the parking lot.
- Most students are at least 100 feet away from the guardsmen. Joseph Lewis is the closest person to the guard except for those on the patio adjacent to Taylor Hall.
- The march down and back does not disperse the crowd. Tension increases.
- Most of the students are just spectators watching from the terrace of Taylor Hall. Joe Lewis is 20 yards from John Cleary. Joe Cullum is further back.
- The guardsmen wheel and shoot in unison, as if on cue. Their fire is generally aimed at the parking lot, not toward the terrace where most of the students are watching.
- Members of the company fire into the air. General Canterbury, in a suit and gas mask, moves forward and orders the shooting stopped.

Postscript:

- General Canterbury later testified that the guardsmen on the right flank were in danger and that they were justified in firing.
- Alan Canfora believed the guardsmen were picking out targets as they marched up the hill, as they kept looking back.
- Lethal force was used to repress dissent.
- Four students were killed and nine wounded by the Ohio National Guard.
- The Scranton Commission indicated that excessive violence was "unnecessary, unwarranted, and inexcusable."

References

Kifner, J. (June 13, 1970). Regrets are few in Kent, Ohio. *The New York Times*.
McCullough, D., Gaffney, E., & Howe, B. R. (1999). The art of biography No. 2. *The Paris Review, 152*.
Orkland, B. (June 27, 2017). Vietnam '67. *The New York Times*.
Pinar, W. F. (1975). The method of currere. *The American Research Association*.
Pinar, W. F. (2017). That first year. *Currere Exchange Journal, 1*(1), 1–10.

2 History and Currere

If one could hop back in time to 1970, the city and university would look roughly the same. Students in bell bottoms and miniskirts hurry to class. Elongated automobiles without airbags and catalytic converters take you places, and attendants pump gas at stations with names like *Sohio*. Some of the downtown restaurants and bars are still there, but a new gentrified shopping and eatery area has replaced most of them. There might be some temporal shock seeing Route 59 as a two-lane highway. A bridge built in 1977 spanning the railroad tracks and the Cuyahoga River is still in the planning stage. As a result, traffic flow and schedules are often disrupted by the pervasive trains. Lawson's stores dot Northeast Ohio, and Richard Nixon has been sworn in as president. Some bars have go-go dancers who "interpret" the music through dance.

On Water Street, an eatery invites breakfast conversations in its cramped quarters.

There are a limited number of people who were on campus during this tragedy and fewer who will talk about it. Reports are plentiful in the archives and online from a cross-section of students and professors. These vernacular reports work well with the method of currere and narrative form. They invite a telling, the fresh testimony developing a picture of what happened on May 4, 1970. We have the advantage of seeing things in now-time, with the accompanying perspectives and insights. It is a compelling subject, and I'm interested in both the recounting of what happened and the educational journeys of the persons who were *there*. They have generously taken me to their world of 1970 as a vicarious time traveler, and I am grateful.

Not including many of the professors, authority figures were generally incompetent or mean-spirited. Given the circumstances and outcomes, this isn't hard to defend. As evidenced by the response from the police, guardsmen, Governor Rhodes, and Mayor Satrom, students were wounded and killed needlessly. Then and now, it is risky to assume that because people hold these positions, they will use their authority in a responsible manner. Kent State president Robert I. White was conveniently out of town, giving university control to the National Guard.

10 *History and Currere*

Figure 2.1 Taken on May 3, 1970, an Army Jeep travels westbound and a 1967 station wagon eastbound (photograph courtesy of Paul Gailey). In the background: The Prentice Gate and what is now the Kent State University Museum.

Figure 2.2 Jerry's Diner, Kent, Ohio (photo courtesy of the Kent Historical Society). It was described as "a place where artists, musicians, poets and others of questionable repute gather."

The five days leading up to the shootings and the horror of the event itself are also well-documented. The proximity of the shootings to Taylor Hall and the School of Journalism allowed for the accurate reporting of the shootings by forces representing law and order. The tragedy would have been more catastrophic if Professor Glenn Frank hadn't been able to convince the remaining seated 200 students to leave because General Canterbury and the guard were ready to advance again. Orders were given to shoot if the demonstrators didn't disperse. The National Guard was assembled and ready, at port arms with loaded weapons. I believe this event needs to be revisited with a different approach using the *Method of Currere* and interviews that might be called *psychoanalytic guided regression*. The Method of Currere is a postmodern approach to education with psychoanalytic underpinnings as described by William Pinar but is not to be considered therapy. It encourages self-exploration, and the journey has been to reach out to those who directly experienced May 4, 1970. This writing is the outcome of that inquiry, discovery, and reflection.

The shootings at Kent State University effectively closed out the 1960s. It seemed like a betrayal to those who believed that President Nixon would honor his pledge – his "secret plan" – to end the war in Vietnam. On April 30, 1970, Nixon announced on television that he was expanding the war into Cambodia. There was an uproar, and the following day, campus demonstrations were occurring all over the country. Two demonstrations were held at Kent State on the Commons. The Commons is a verdant, open expanse down the hill from Taylor Hall. Bordered by the hills, a heating plant, and Engleman Hall, it formed a natural amphitheater. The Victory Bell figured prominently near the hill and looks roughly the same today. During commemorations, the stage is set up facing the hill. Voices and music are gently amplified and refracted, suspended for a moment in mid-air. On May 4, 1970, student voices were strident as they buried the Constitution during the demonstration. A National Guard jeep drove past with a bullhorn, ordering the students to disperse. They were under the command of Brigadier General Robert Canterbury, and tear gas was fired using M79 grenade launchers. Students began throwing the canisters back at the guard. The students were forced to retreat up and over Blanket Hill. What followed was a violent and deadly suppression at 12:24 p.m.

A month later, the supergroup Crosby, Stills, Nash, and Young released their anthem "Ohio," but what did it really mean? What good did it do? For many, there was disillusionment, a tendency toward apathy and hopelessness. President Nixon, Vice President Spiro T. Agnew, Governor Rhodes, and Mayor Satrom prevailed, and we were resigned to living in a country that sanctioned violence against unarmed students on their own campus. Perhaps this was modernism resurfacing, insidiously reappearing in a world that seemed inherently violent. There were two ways to look at the events and the nation. From the right, we often heard *Love it or leave it*. From the left, it was *Fix it or f*** it*. There wasn't much of a middle ground. For students my age, there was a malaise, a feeling that things were not well, an existential crisis.

There were two ways to interpret this disquiet and horror following May 4, 1970. One path offered disillusionment, the other a small measure of hope for the future: Enchanted violence associates death with generative power; in this formulation, death may hold the promise of rebirth or of the emergence of new meaning or the possibility of transformative power. With disenchanted violence, however, such power is rejected, and death is recast as insignificant or meaningless: "any illusions and ideals about the dead or injured body's being generative are stripped away and often dismissed as an additional violation" (Outka, 2015, p. 313).

In the face of the reality – the killings at Kent State – the violence may be described as sometimes having transformative outcomes. May 4 may well represent pain and trauma as a transcendental experience.

The enormity of physical and emotional pain surrounding May 4 make the subject inexhaustible. Sarah Cole describes the work of literature in addressing modernist violence:

> Easter 1916 is a glorious beginning, as is Masada, and in the ruins of Troy Virgil conjures the seeds of Rome. In *The Aeneid*, it is a band of ragged survivors who eventually will found the empire.
> (Cole, 2012, p. 4)

She sees violence as a recurring, inherited story in culture and religion, repeated in war and violent events. Modernist literature took up classical myth and "heroic wanderers" (Cole, p. 4) as a point of origin, and not necessarily a triumphant beginning.

Initially, Modernist writers addressed violence during and following World War I (called *The Great War* at the time). If there is a *yin and yang* embodied in the stories presented here, it is that there may have been – and will be – positive outcomes that push back against shameful cultural and institutional violence. The persons I've interviewed have arrived at an acceptance (or at least, acknowledgment) of the trauma they've experienced and taken steps to address it.

Modernism was a global phenomenon, not contained within the United States. This emerged as an alignment with the values of industrial life in the early 20th century. Modernism had a great effect on historians, teachers, and learners. It surfaced in many areas, including literature and education. The Enlightenment and industrial age were symptomatic of modernism until World War II. Modernist individualism – the individual triumphing over obstacles thanks to reason, capitalism, and self-absorption. It called to mind Ayn Rand's *The Fountainhead* and *Atlas Shrugged*. Societal concerns are secondary, an early form of neoliberal thought. Modernity as applies to education is both Eurocentric and invested in management and accountability. For example, following Nixon's election to the presidency, he began the "Back to Basics" program. Unveiled in March of 1970 in a speech, this educational reform was an integral component of Nixon's domestic policy. He created the National Institute of Education (NIE)o oversee the whole thing. It was a political move, mollifying white voters who disliked social reforms granted to people of color while attempting to provide better access to education as part of the mythical "American Dream."

Postmodern perspectives emerged as a response to modernism's shortcomings. As an example, when I began teaching, behavioral objectives were the dominant paradigm for politicians and administrators. The modernist perspective was management by objectives, behavioral steps, and assessments. The educator was embroiled in writing goals and tying assessments to them. In this climate, the teacher was reduced from artist to facilitator. This modernism as applied to curriculum theory has roots in the work of early theorists. Franklin Bobbitt published his seminal book entitled *The Curriculum* in 1918, the summer when my maternal grandmother graduated from Classical High School. This set the stage for Ralph Tyler's *Eight-Year Study* and what is commonly known as the *Tyler Rationale*. The groundwork for "scientism" approach began with Bobbitt and his reliance on accountability and management came from Frederick Winslow Taylor. Taylor originally studied factory assembly line management, and this eventually became part of teaching and learning in public schools. Reinforced by Ralph Tyler and the *Rationale*, this was critiqued by Dwayne Huebner and Herbert Kliebard during the 1960s. Tyler's rationale represents the curriculum field's historical commitment to curriculum development. It serves as an "organizing symbol and normative referent for the way that curriculum development –everything from lesson planning to program designing, to student evaluation – should be conceived and practiced" (Henderson, 2015, p. 23). The Tyler Rationale resulted in excessive standardization. The societal perspective, both in the country and the schools, was dominated by black-and-white thinking. It was a bleak affair, and is still in evidence today.

William Doll Jr. offered the following historical perspective to address the underpinnings of the *Tyler Rationale*: "In recent years I have seen the Rationale not so much as a model to be challenged but rather as an expression of a particular time, a modernist time, now past" (Doll, 2012, p. 3). Post-modernism was emerging in many disciplines, including "Reconstructionist" curriculum theorists like William Pinar and Madeleine Grumet. The postmodern perspective in teaching, learning, and curriculum studies is tied directly to the Reconceptualists of the 1970s, especially in conjunction with William Pinar and the method of *currere*. Notions of modernist trust and faith in both our leaders and curriculum studies dissolved and curriculum workers began to fill the empty space. Within the field, there was pushback to the educational scientism of the 1950s and 1960s through problem-solving, educational leadership, and curriculum study. At the same time, Herbert Kliebard was declaring the curriculum field moribund, theorists like Dwayne Huebner and James B. MacDonald offered hope. They opened a door and the Recoceptualists were able to walk through it. This might be understood as a nonlinear engagement with history, a new way of seeing. Nonadherence to science and rational "modern" paradigms of knowing and being – epistemology and ontology – became a form of transcendence, a "course to be run." This is what the *Method of Currere* offers through a four-phased process: regressive, progressive, analytic, and synthetic. Whether the modern world and worldview provided an opportunity for a tragedy is likely, but speculative. I've allowed allow the interviewees to tell their stories and share their currere journeys. As a democratic gesture, the reader is free to interpret, analyze, and formulate their own syntheses.

Huebner was a professor at Columbia University. His insights deconstructed educational goals, purposes, and objectives as facile, replacing the need for an awareness of historicity. He searched for "continuity" in the present, past, and future, not the ahistoricism inherent in unambiguous goals:

> It serves almost the same function to those over twenty-six that drugs serve for the younger – tune in, turn on, drop out. To find the purpose for schools is thought to restore the calm and enable educators to drop out of the troublesome political process of living historically. It has almost been assumed that if the educator can clearly state his goal, then he has fulfilled the responsibilities as an historical being. But historical responsibility is much too complex to be so easily dismissed. It is too easy to forget that debate about educational objectives is part of the continuous struggle of rival political ideologies.
>
> (Huebner, 1987, p. 325)

Please read his words again. They are visionary, providing a glimpse into the future of curriculum work. Huebner's endorsement of historical awareness relies upon the component of political action through curriculum work. This reactivation of history is valuable work for both society and the curriculum. The testimonies highlight the graphic record of May 4, and in doing so, they serve as history, deepening the embarrassment of what happened, a necessary first step in pointing to better futures.

The persons I've interviewed possess a wealth of information. They were *there*. They've earned the right to tell their stories, with memories, perspectives, and insights securely grounded in their past experiences at Kent State. They are connected to the things that existed in that world, a world they should be allowed to see through a visual, nonlinear, nonrational, and spiritual lens. Those characteristics might be considered vital elements of a postmodern perspective. Learning that occurs is not tied to external, rational, and scientific modern paradigms. It is interpretive. It is likely that modernist paradigms allowed – or contributed to – the tragedy that unfolded on campus in 1970. The modernist external, top-down management sensibilities weren't tied to what the 1960s were beginning to embody. There was a counterculture, and many of us believed that higher planes of thinking and behavior existed. There was an optimism – however naïve – that peace, love, and spirituality were here to stay. Astronauts had walked on the moon; there were negotiations to minimize nuclear bomb threats; the standard of living was rising. Many began college in the late 1960s, young people hoping to make a difference. We didn't know what this entailed but were excited to leave the convergent education of the public schools and move into critical, creative engagement through liberal studies. My freshman year concluded with May 4, 1970.

Instead of this optimism, disillusionment replaced hope on May 4. There were other urgent problems lurking in dark corners: "The war in the Vietnamese quagmire drags on. Black rage is bitter. A segment of the young revolt or drop out. The 'silent majority' hardens its attitude towards dissent" (Van Til, 1970, p. 345). This hardening emerged full force in Kent as state-sanctioned violence. The students were abandoned by the administration on that day as the National Guard was allowed to take over the campus. Many in the local community agreed with the response. As the students walked out of town, some locals held up four fingers representing the dead while shouting insults. Editorials in the *Record-Courier* the following day praised the guard for their response. A comment from a community leader reflected the prevailing attitude: "It's a shame it had to take killing to do it, but all those kids were someplace they shouldn't have been" said Dick Richards, a florist lunching at the weekly meeting of the Lions Club at the Brown Derby, just outside of town" (Flint, 1970). This kind of polarizing rhetoric is evident in the United States even today. As a result, the lessons of May 4 are more relevant than ever. Unfortunately, in the present-day, conspiracy theories and innuendo are accelerated by social media platforms.

This is tied to the curriculum field in ways we might not have initially imagined. At that time, James G. Henderson – professor emeritus from Kent State – was a student of Elliot Eisner. He "integrates three influential interpretations of curriculum – curriculum as deliberative artistry, curriculum as complicated conversation, and curriculum as *currere* – with John Dewey's lifetime work on reflective inquiry. At its core, it advances *a way of studying* as *a way of living* with reference to the question: How might I live as a democratic educator?" (Henderson, 2016, p. i). But what manner of educational journey unfolded on May 4, 1970? Are they moments that may inspire? Perhaps there are flakes of gold to be gleaned through their words. My interviewees and the country at large witnessed an unparalleled injustice. Henderson writes,

16 *History and Currere*

There are moments that inspire me to grow as a professional. "Teachable moments" and positive experiences certainly give a sense of clarity to my work. However, these moments of injustice that cause a visceral anger in my being are the ones that truly engender change in my practice. Winfield (2007) cautions that when we are most comfortable is when injustices and its underlying "ideology operates in its most pernicious state".

(Henderson et al., 2015, p. 6)

There may be teachable moments in the visceral anger surrounding the fourth of May. The violence against students on their own campus embodies this pernicious state. As curriculum workers, it was necessary to confront our collective past, including the war in Vietnam and the shootings at Kent State University. Please consider Picasso's majestic and awe-inspiring *Guernica*, a response to the atrocities of the Spanish Civil War. It is a majestic and powerful anti-war statement in oil. The world is represented allegorically as looking in – horrified – with an illuminating lantern. There exists only one image of hope: a severed arm and broken sword with an emergent flower. Kent State University was the stage upon which history pivoted and – eventually – was reimagined and reborn. It developed its own history and symbolic images. One of these images was a photograph taken by John Filo. It found iconic status embodied by what Jerry M. Lewis calls the *Kent State Pieta*.

In 1970, *everyone* my age was affected by the Vietnam War. During our lifetimes, the United States had been perpetually at war in Indochina. Whether by proxy or directly, 45,000 American troops were killed in what is now called *The Vietnam War*. A narrative history with documentation was leaked to the New York Times, and they began to be published on June 13, in 1971:

> On June 17, 1967, at a time of great personal disenchantment with the war, Robert S. McNamara, who was then Secretary of Defense, made what may turn out to be one of the most important decisions in his seven years at the Pentagon. He commissioned what has become known as the Pentagon papers – a massive top-secret history of the United States role in Indochina.
>
> (p. ix, The Pentagon Papers)

The Kent State shootings occurred in front of the journalism building and are therefore well-documented by iconic photographs and testimony of the guard advancing with tear gas, ascending the hill, marching to the practice field, retreating, turning, and shooting. The eyewitness accounts presented here assist the reader with multiple perspectives, and multiple ways of processing what happened. We see how they perceived the occurrences in the first person.

This horrific event resulted in student protests across the country, ultimately helping to end the war in Vietnam. The interviews, analysis, and syntheses incorporate a new approach using focusing on the psychoanalytic component of currere and a *guided regression*. This is not a form of therapy, but rather interviews and reflections through the method of currere. I believe that the subject remains relevant to those who were living at the time, and those who came after. For those who came after. For all of us, the threat of violence and political suppression remains in the United States 52 years later. As a means of study, events are seen as educational experiences, using the hypothesis that "at any given moment he or she is in a biographic situation" (Pinar & Grumet, 1976, p. 51). Their biographies as they were/are/ lived enjoin the past and present to point toward possible futures. But they must "go back," generating data by revisiting the past. This is accomplished through the regressive stage of currere.

In the regressive step, lived and existential experiences become a data source. To generate this "data," one free associates, after the psychoanalytic technique, to recall the past, reconstructing, enlarging, and transforming the meanings. Madeleine Grumet describes *currere* as an attempt to "reveal the ways that histories (both collective and individual) and hope suffuse our moments, and to study them through telling our stories of educational experience" (Grumet, 1981, p. 118).

The (relative) safety of the present makes possible regressive access to educational experiences, and not necessarily in isolation. The autobiographical telling expands their experiences into a larger forum, giving voice – meaning – as they communicate with others. This process and these concepts have their beginnings with a high school teacher during the 1960s.

William Pinar has written about his early years of teaching on Long Island and taking the train into New York for a class with Dwayne Huebner. While not describing him as perfect or godlike, there is a reverence in his descriptions of Dr. Huebner. He recounts sitting in a large room with others in the profession, hinging on every word the distant figure in front is sharing. In an introduction to *The Lure of the Transcendent*, Pinar emphasizes the use of language, history of the field, "other possible stories and renewing vision" (Huebner, 1999, p. xi). In keeping with the pursuit of higher ideals, I'm hoping that this writing reactivates history and renews our vision through narratives that inform May 4. The stories, currere, and biographic sketches are the humanizing *soul* of the writing: "Humanization in the tradition of Paulo Freire is, "the process of becoming more fully human as social, historical, thinking, communicating, transformative, creative persons who participate in and with the world" (Salazar, 2013, p. 126).

Historiography, Biography, Memoir

In beginning with a discussion about historiography, biography, and memoir, it's valuable to look at memory and curriculum as pertaining to May 4. I recently reached out to Petra Hendry, and she offered the following suggestions: "Karl, the last chapter in Engendering Curriculum History speaks to nature of curriculum as nonlinear, relational and as an ethics. This might be helpful for thinking through some ideas. The introduction as well talks about history as curriculum histories from a poststructural perspective" (Petra Munro Hendry, personal communication, October 7, 2022).

Petra Hendry channels the Greek poet Sappho and the desire to be remembered by future generations. She suggests that remembrance is vital, necessary, and beneficial to effect positive change in the present. In this manner, history is not forgotten, and there is hope that the future will result in new understandings of knowledge: "[T]he role of memory is not one of mere remembering, but one of reorganization. Re-membering is a relational ethics that connects us across space and time to those ties that remind us of our humanity" (Hendry, 2011, p. 207).

Stated another way, there is more to the story than a structuralist concrete reality on one hand and ephemeral ideas and concepts on the other. The poststructuralist approach might look at the "object" itself and the systems that manufactured that object. As pertaining to May 4, poststructuralism in education emerged in the mid-1960s and continued through the 1970s. It encourages discourse about wealth and privilege, knowledge and control, and sees "truth" as interpretive. This is particularly valuable when May 4 is an object of discussion. There is even a book by Peter Davies entitled *The Truth About Kent State: A Challenge to the American Conscience* (1973). Reviewed in the *New York Times*, his purpose was described as limited and focused: "He seeks only to remind us that justice cannot have been done where legal authorities have demonstrated so little interest in the simple truth" (Powers, 1973, para 10). The Scranton Commission reported that the shootings had been "unnecessary, unwarranted and inexcusable." Before Vice President Agnew pleaded no contest to income tax evasion and resigned, he dismissed their findings as "pablum for permissiveness, and the President ignored their recommendations" (Powers, para 12).

Alan Canfora dedicated a lifetime to uncovering the truth about May 4, hoping for a National Guard deathbed confession. His questions generally remained unanswered, and Thomas Powers suggests that a conspiracy to fire in unison was "plausible." If not truth, plausibility hovers and orbits around it. This is valuable as pointing to a likelihood because we know the primary truth: General Canterbury decided to forcibly disperse a legal and peaceful rally on the students' own campus, and human life was considered disposable.

But where are humanity, compassion, and empathy in the history of Kent State? Perhaps it's to be found through curriculum scholarship and theorizing surrounding the May 4 narratives and analyses. The course of the country was altered by the events of May 4, and my intent is to remember and reactivate the events of May 4, 1970, at Kent State University. In revisiting what happened, new knowledge and perspectives may be generated, in the process uncovering elements of our humanity. William Pinar offers some guidance for this journey: "The opposite of arrest, to activate means to vitalize, to breathe life into, and be breathed into life. Reactivating the past is engagement with alterity – specifically with the singularity of the past in its distinctive complexity – that sets in motion, well, we can't know" (Pinar, 2014, p. 7). It is that hopeful ambiguity which drives this *currere* narrative, that positive change and insights will be engendered and set in motion.

The Greeks

Petra Hendry has incorporated the Greeks into her arguments, and I will attempt the same. With regard to narrative, there may be a process of healing through storytelling. Scholars like to frame their inquiries as a journey, suggesting that the process is weighted more heavily than the product – the result. The method of currere is emblematic of that paradigm, a "course to be run." My personal journey of inquiry to tell this story has been in creative ferment for decades. Initially, I was looking for the truth – or truths – that hover around and about what transpired, i.e., what "happened." Professor Frank X. Ryan suggests that philosophy is uncooperative and recalcitrant as a tool for uncovering truth: Traditionally, philosophy's raison d'etre has been the search for immutable truth, the quest for certainty. There is, naturally, no agreement about what would constitute such a secure foundation" (Ryan, 2011, p. 3). He recommends instead a more broad, ecological perspective, dedicated to creative problem-solving. As a Deweyan, transactional tool, his circuit of inquiry may give us objective facts and values to be examined, resulting in hypotheses subject to future inquiries. Life experiences such as the survivors of May 4 experienced may result in hypotheses and syntheses to be put to the test, subject to ongoing review, and not as self-evident truths. Ryan (2011) suggests that fact is interpretive and transactional: "That what is known as fact is inseparable from how we determine it to be so. In support of this, Dewey and Bentley cite the original Latin root of fact, *factum*, as something done or made" (p. 51). My journey, my inquiry, has been to gather the stories and interpretations of eyewitness experience and distill what may be considered an "object" – a Deweyan object of inquiry. Through currere these findings inform what they teach us about learning and doing and being. This is my intent. Recently, I sat down with Greek scholar Rick Newton, and the following insights are what we distilled from the conversation.

Regarding journeys, were their ever stories so epic as those described by Homer? We are enlightened as to the healing of Ulysses' injured heart. (The line is Iliad 9.189.) Achilles is "delighting his heart" by playing his lyre and singing "the famous deeds of men" (war stories of heroes who have won eternal memory in such songs as the Iliad itself). Rick believes the scene is "self-referential," alluding perhaps to Homer, whose songs bestow immortality (in terms of human memory) on warriors.

A stringed instrument played and prized by the ancient Greeks, Hermes was credited as the lyre's inventor, and a plectrum of bone was used to strum or pick. Playing the lyre to make music was an important component of education in Greece. Depicted extensively on ancient coins, Achilles was reputedly taught to play by a centaur named Cheiron.

This lyre in particular that Achilles played was a reward for sacking Thebes. That same victory also won him Briseis (daughter of Briseus), whom Agamemnon took from him. This seizure enraged Achilles and caused him to leave the Trojan expedition. This is what engendered his wrath. He takes his Myrmidons with him, nursing his rage in his tent. He uses narrative through his voice, singing his story.

1 Narrative can soothe an injured soul: Achilles "was charming/delighting/soothing his spirit" by singing tales of heroic and memorable exploits. Storytelling was used as therapy or, at least, an analgesic.
2 The fact that Achilles is singing tales "of men" and not just of himself suggests that the very genre of the narrative (here, epic) can contribute to healing. Achilles can contextualize his personal trauma with stories of others. Every warrior had his own "cycle" of famous exploits: Achilles is just one of many.

 When Agamemnon took Briseis in Book 1, Achilles's response was to act out and narcissistically attach to his wound. By Book 9, he had broadened his perspective. He is still not over it by Book 9, but he is a work in progress.

 (In terms of narrative therapy, a person's very choice of genre can be informative. It depends on whether they call the story a tragedy, comedy, romance, short story, sonnet, or epic).
3 The fact that the lyre was included with Briseis suggests a correlation between the main prize itself (Briseis) and the instrument (lyre) for constructing the narrative. You cannot have a song without a lyre, so the narrative might serve as a substitute – a surrogate – for the actual issue or event.

 The source of the wound (Briseis from the sack of Thebes) provides the source of the therapy (lyre). The self-healing narrator must go to the very source of the wound to find and create the cure. "A narrative cure is, by definition, a construct. But it must adhere closely and faithfully to the facts. It cannot be a lie" (Rick Newton, personal communication, December 11, 2022).

4   Self-referentially, Achilles becomes a version of Homer himself – the lyre/strumming singer of the entire Iliad. This is significant in the discussion of memory. The poet only remembers events that are central to his narrative. The rest is omitted as irrelevant. Therefore, a poet's memory is selective. Also selective is that of the hero, the protagonist who remembers some details but not others. Homer is the ultimate storyteller, and he must rely on the *Muses* to keep his story together:

"The mother of the Muses was Mnemosyne, Memory herself! A true narrator is the controller – / not the victim – / of memory. This is where 'victim' and 'narratist' converge. In the constructed story, be it epic or tragedy, the narrator emerges as ultimately supreme over the hero. In fact, although Achilles is the hero of the Iliad, there would be no Achilles without a Homer" (Rick Newton, personal communication, December 11, 2022).

A final note: When Achilles sings in his hut, his comrade and friend Patroclus sits across from him and listens. Therefore, every storyteller needs and even requires an audience. It matters *for whom and to whom* the person is telling his story.

The persons I've interviewed *need* to tell their stories, and they *need* an audience. While they speak, I'm in a privileged place, a position of trust. In the absence of Patroclus – Ulysses's childhood friend and comrade in battle – they have the listener or the reader. My responsibility is to convey their words to you. This tragic history *deserves* a new remembrance, reconstructing the sensibilities of those who listen to their stories. I've chosen to revisit events that promise a "difficult return" (Pinar, 2014, p. 9). It is a remembrance of the tragedy of May 4, understanding history through currere explorations of persons who were in the line of fire on campus on that Monday of May 4. It is a difficult return for the interviewees, but – like Achilles in his hut – perhaps contextualizing their trauma with the stories contributes to a "healing" of the soul.

The Curriculum

But how does this connect with the curriculum? Curriculum theory is more than establishing objectives, instruction, and evaluation. William Pinar defines curriculum as a "complicated conversation." Following that, theorizing the history of May 4, 1970, as curriculum is both complicated and difficult. The purpose here is to reactivate the past, to breathe life into those horrific events, a vital complicated conversation. Through this conversation, I hope to generate some answers to the question "How could this have happened" from people who were *there* and delve into some curriculum theory. After the first step of regression (and they don't have to be completed in order) using the Method of Currere, it is hoped that the progressive, analytic, and synthetic phases will generate new knowledge. In the past and even today, there is a tendency toward immediacy, a narcissistic kind of ahistoricism. At Kent State, it was illustrated through the administration's desire to "move on," to distance itself from its traumatic history. The May 4 Task Force did not allow this to happen. As May 4 approached, university administrators and townspeople perennially suggested they "get over it." However, the past two presidents, Beverly J. Warren (July 2014–July 2019) and Todd Diacon (July 2019–present), have acknowledged ownership of the university's past, supportive of the ongoing work. They've even gone so far as to Roseann "Chic" Canfora to teach in the School of Media and Journalism. A previous *persona non grata*, she now serves on the Office of the President as chair of the May 4 Presidential Advisory Committee.

Alistair Begg believes that history matters, that y*our* history matters:

> You are, to some significant degree, who you are because of who your parents were and who your grandparents were. You can't disassociate yourself from that. You are the product of that lineage. And it matters. Now, I say that to you because we live in an environment in which history is debunked at the highest academic levels of our nation. Those who teach history in the Ivy League schools, who are the proponents of history, are at pains to teach their pupils that there is no history that is knowable – that we cannot know history in any pure form. Because, after all, we view history through the clouded lens of our own circumstances and presuppositions and so on. Therefore, it is impossible for us to know history.
>
> (Alistair Begg, 2001)

He is a theorist and theologian and believes that the Bible is a historical document and that Christ is a historical figure. The text written 200 years after the death of Christ is relevant if you haven't debunked the whole notion of history. This presupposes that there *is* – in fact – *a* "knowable history." even if we believe that history is unknowable. Whether unknowable or not, the history of May 4, 1970, is important, worthy of revisiting. New generations of activists believe so, and so do I. There is a mystery that you can *feel* on the Commons, Taylor Hall, or the parking lot. If the history isn't pure and unfettered, it *matters*. History is a messy endeavor, likewise curriculum theorizing. In the past decade, there has been a reluctant acknowledgment and ownership by Kent State University Presidents Todd Diacon and Beverly Warren. Getting to this point is an example of what William Pinar has labeled a "complicated conversation." It may be impossible to know and understand the history of May 4, but no matter. However one interprets those events, the history isn't going away.

Mark Twain was reported to have remarked, "History never repeats itself, but it does often rhyme." This temporal concept played out repeatedly. Kent State is part of history to many, but to individuals my age, it is part of who we are as people. This affected us locally and on a societal level. Violence was, and is, pervasive and cyclical. The late 1960s were rife with the violent suppression of activists against the war in Indochina. This only resulted in an overpouring of anger. For example, on March 24, 1970, a bomb was detonated at the base of Rodin's *The Thinker*, at the Cleveland Museum of Art. "It was reported that this attack was undertaken by a radical political group, perhaps as a commentary on the continuing military action in Vietnam or the elitism of the American government" (*The Thinker Vandalized*).

The optimism of the Vietnam War was withering due to the Tet Offensive and American atrocities. It seemed unwinnable. Martin Luther King was killed by a racist in Memphis, and urban centers were shut down by race riots, with many cities engulfed in violence. Robert Kennedy was thereafter assassinated in a Los Angeles hotel by Sirhan Sirhan. Whatever fault lines that divided "us" from "them" are still evident today. Violence and race weren't only Southern issues. An iconic photograph from "busing" conflicts of the 1970s shows a white Bostonian attempting to run a black man through with an American flag.

It wasn't solely a Republican issue. Hubert Horatio Humphrey was handed the Democratic nomination as demonstrators were violently subdued by Mayor Richard J. Daley and the Chicago police. The 1968 election of Richard Nixon set the stage for sweeping changes in the United States. Known as the *Southern* Strategy, it marginalized people of color by attacking integration and civil rights. Nixon's call for "law and order" spilled over into authoritarian management of demonstrations, dissent, and even education. This was also evident in Governor Rhodes's response to the activism at Kent State. As Chic Canfora has pointed out, many in the town, state, and country wish that the history would remain dormant, but it needs to be reexplored. The history – the public memory of May 4 – remains a disputed and polarizing space.

In over five decades, "efforts to commemorate and memorialize the shootings at Kent State have generated continuing controversy. Public or official memory of these events remains contested for the simple reason that it has proven extremely difficult to achieve agreement on what 'May 4th' and 'Kent State' mean" (Weldes & Laffey, 2001, p. 4). This is especially relevant today considering the resurgence of state-sanctioned violence not only on the local level but also nationally:

> When you couple this militarization of law enforcement with an erosion of civil liberties and due process that allows the police to become judge and jury – national security letters, no-knock searches, broad

24 *History and Currere*

general warrants, pre-conviction forfeiture – we begin to have a very serious problem on our hands. Given these developments, it is almost impossible for many Americans not to feel like their government is targeting them.

(Rand Paul, 2014)

As a brief review, on April 30, 1970, President Nixon announced the invasion of Cambodia on national television, reversing his campaign promises regarding "Vietnamization" of the Vietnam War. On college campuses everywhere, students protested the escalation of the war. Subsequently, 13 Kent State students were shot on May 4, four fatally. Images were on television around the world by that evening. John Filo's photograph of Mary Ann Vecchio screaming over the body of Jeffrey Miller immediately became an emblem larger than the image itself. It became iconic, what Jerry M. Lewis has called the *Kent State Pieta* (Jerry Lewis, personal communication, March 15, 2021).

This disturbing image has become part of the historical "collective" memory of Kent State. Filo's photograph taken from the front – a closer vantage point – is much more graphic. It's hard to believe that much blood could drain out of a person, a foot-wide stream contrasting with the sunny pavement. What, exactly, does this theoretical "collective memory" entail? For Emile Durkheim, "totems and rites" bequeath importance that affects

Figure 2.3 Mary Ann Vecchio kneeling over the body of Jeffrey Miller. (photograph by John Filo, courtesy of Getty Images and Kent State University).

the collective consciousness and memory. In speaking of rites as "glorious souvenirs" that give men strength and confidence, Durkheim frames the importance of invoking the ritual attitude through representations" (p. 420). In theory, we are allowed to "go back" – regress – to the past and see what it represents, and future positive changes engendered. John Filo's photograph is itself an icon, an iconic image that invites discourse, remembrance, constructions, and reconstructions of what happened – and why.

- Regarding *public memory*, images of May 4 such as *The Pagoda* or Don Drumm's *Solar Totem* haven't been allowed to become invisible. They patiently wait for spring and reactivation through commemorative activities. They weren't placed there after the fact. They *became* "important" as structures in public memory because they weren't allowed to slip into the unconscious, to fade into a kind of anonymity. They stand unchanged, except that the Drumm sculpture with the M1 bullet hole is continually drawn upon with chalk and has been since 1970 (see Figure 2.4). Don Drumm refused to have it "repaired" after the shootings, believing that it should stand as a testimonial. General Canterbury and Governor Rhodes believed that the activists fired the first shot because the burr was facing the guard. Not so. Don Drumm set up a similar piece of Cor-ten steel and fired an M1 rifle at it, disproving their claims. The National Guard fired without provocation by unfriendly fire. The other memorial plaques and structures were erected later, upon approval from the university administration.
- Conflict has centered on the commemorations (the most important ones happening on the "fives" and the "zeros"), ongoing dialogue, and even the need for public monuments on campus at all. If conservative,

Figure 2.4 Close up of Don Drumm's *Solar Totem # 1* at Kent State University, January, 1978 (Photograph courtesy of William Coglano).

you might believe that the students had moved from protest into anarchy through the breaking of windows and burning of the dilapidated ROTC building. The breaking of a promise by President Nixon would not have been an excuse for "rioting." If you believed that those events should be part of ongoing public memory, then you would endorse the plans for memorials.

Memorializing

Iconic photographic images may memorialize, becoming what we would label "public memory." During the 1970s and 1980s, there were attempts at establishing permanent memorials on the Commons and in the parking lot adjacent to Prentice Hall. Sculptures and statues were considered, among them a bronze *Abraham and Isaac*, a realistic portrayal of the moment in the Bible before a father kills his son. It was roundly rejected as "too violent." But what place do statuary, and even photographic images, have in public memory?

"[O]bjects such as statues are put in place to secure memory – not just any memory, but one that serves the interests of a particular group and its ideology, or view of itself and the events that it assembles in the stories that the group celebrates" (Morgan, 2018, p. 4). As an example, a Confederate statue dedicated in 1913 at the University of North Carolina dubbed *Silent Sam* was pulled down in 2018 and now rests in the library archives. To many, it represented white supremacy and slavery. The conflict played out in 2018 with the statue being pulled down by activists. Is this not like the burning of the ROTC building, a generally hated reminder of the ongoing war in Vietnam? There surely are deep rifts in our cultural sensibilities and history, and these fissures continue to the present day in narratives celebrated by opposing points of view. The May 4 commemorations are remembrances that promote shared ways of thinking.

The sculptures, objects, and even buildings and parking lots themselves have become shrine-like. They are invisible to many, but their presence is seen and felt. Permanent signage offers didactic for a visitor to ponder, ready to be annually reactivated into life. Intense feelings may be engendered, but questions remain:

> With these remarks on the form and content of public memory in mind, how is it that so many of the statues in city parks commemorating heroes and wars so easily fade into the background? What is their status as material objects.
>
> (p. 155)

The conflicts that played out during the past two years in the South reveal the instability of historical narratives and the important role that objects perform in attempting to anchor them. The objects offer access to the past, but only through the window of the present (p. 155). A good number of people who grew up in the South remain furious about the removal of Confederate statuary and the Battle Flag from public areas. Discussion and conversation are off the table, including any talk about related issues such as the *1619 Project*. At Kent State, the university is beginning to acknowledge its past, reluctantly taking ownership of the history.

Hannah Arendt

Hannah Arendt described the banality of evil she experienced while reporting on the trial of Eichmann in Jerusalem: "However monstrous the deeds were, the doer was neither monstrous nor demonic, and the only specific characteristic one could detect in his past as well as in his behavior during the trial and the preceding police examination was something entirely negative: It was not stupidity but a curious, quite authentic inability to think" (Arendt, 1971, p. 417). She was severely criticized for these reflections, but her motives were genuine. Atrocities may emerge from mindless conscription to duty, clearly evident in the killings of May 4, 1970.

Please consider the military mindset of Company G of the Ohio National Guard. Inconsistencies and contradictions during cross-examination. Was it intentional evildoing as they squeezed the trigger or just an absence of thought? Again, from Arendt's lecture: "Do the ability to think and a disastrous failure of what we commonly call conscience coincide? The very word *con-science*, at any rate, points in this direction insofar as it means 'to know with and by myself,' a kind of knowledge that is actualized in every thinking process" (Arendt, 1971, p. 418). If military units – trained soldiers – are deployed on a campus with unarmed students, is there *any* sort of positive outcome that may be envisioned? Very few, but the opposite is likely. Three things can happen, and two of them are bad. Militarized units do not think – they are trained to take orders, not reliant on conscience. Many local townspeople thought the response was correct, that the students should not have assembled and "*got what was coming to them.*"

The Annex

The *Move the Gym* controversy of 1977–1978 was an attempt at commemoration in the preservation of the original site. The university decided to build a gymnasium, and this brought a larger focus into the continuing dialogue. The candlelight walks and vigils were individual, centered on the loss of life and injuries. Something more than an annual living memorial would be required. Weldes and Laffey (2001) opined that building the annex, i.e., the *new gym*, would cover up the *truth* about May 4, obscuring the distances that the shootings involved:

> As determined by the FBI and made public in the President's Commission on Campus Unrest (hereafter the Scranton Commission Report), many of the students shot – and all of those killed – were quite a distance from the Guard, and often not facing the guardsmen at all.
>
> (p. 14)

If not "covering up" the truth, the new construction would obscure the fact through a distorted scale the proximity of the students to the National Guard. This was presented by the speakers on August 20, 1970, including the parents of the killed and injured students. Especially poignant was the appearance of Joan Baez, adding weight and authenticity to the event while connecting the ongoing issues to previous histories of the 1960s, the ongoing struggles for remembrance, connecting the past and present, and laying the groundwork for the future.

Gregory and Lewis (1988) describe the challenges faced by the historian, sociologist, poet, and even curriculum theorist as not fitting arbitrarily into a prescribed slot. The structuralist influence and the importance of origins structure the present-day:

> Schwartz's inference is that the past fits appropriately with the present because in some way the past is structurally the same as the present in that past events set forth the template for all future events. Schwartz (1982) touches upon this notion in an earlier work quoting works of Levi-Strauss.
>
> (p. 215)

From much of the information presented, a culture of ahistoricism has clearly endured over the decades. There are signs of hope. Thanks to the efforts of those I've interviewed, some of the historical dark corners are becoming bright again, illuminated, and visible. They have helped me reactivate the history of Kent State.

And why sweep away the cobwebs? It's valuable to revisit and reconsider May 4 in a critical light, with a call to engage in "complicated conversations." Despite the ongoing issues with state-supported violence, new developments at Kent State are encouraging. For curriculum stakeholders, the field is positively influenced by history, and we can learn from it: "The past is so much more powerful than this paltry (if nightmarish) present" (W. Pinar, personal communication, February 6, 2017). With a conceptualization of the Kent State shootings as curriculum, we study educational and curricular history. With currere and a small measure of hope, we hope to reactivate history and in the process engage in reflection and inquiry.

History and Currere 29

Figure 2.5 Joan Baez, *Move the Gym* concert, August 20, 1977. (photo courtesy of Karl Martin).

References

Arendt, H. (1971). Thinking and moral considerations: A lecture. *Social Research, 38*(3), 417–446.
Cole, S. (2012). *At the violet hour: Modernism and violence in England and Ireland.* Oxford University Press: New York.
Durkheim, Emile (1961). *The elementary forms of the religious life.* Collier Books: New York.
Gregory, S. W., & Lewis, J. M. (1988). Symbols of collective memory: The social process of memorializing May 4, 1970, at Kent State University.
Henderson, J. G., & Colleagues. (2015). *Reconceptualizing curriculum development: Inspiring and informing action.* Routledge: New York, NY.
Huebner, D. (1987). Curriculum as concern for man's temporality. *Theory Into Practice, 26*, 324–331. http://www.jstor.org/stable/1476248
Morgan, D. (2018). Soldier statues and empty pedestals: public memory in the wake of the confederacy. *Material Religion, 14*(1), 153–157.
Outka, E. (2015). Violent Ends, Modernist Means [Review of *At the Violet Hour: Modernism and Violence in England and Ireland*, by S. COLE]. *NOVEL: A Forum on Fiction, 48*(2), 313–316.

Pinar, W. F. (2014). Between hope and despair is resolve: Remembering Roger Simon. *Journal of the Canadian Association for Curriculum Studies*, *11*(2), 6–20.

Pinar, W. F. & Grumet, M. R. (1976). *Toward a poor curriculum*. Kendall-Hunt.

The Pentagon Papers as published by the New York Times (1971) Quadrangle Books, Inc.

Ryan, F. X. (2011) *Seeing together: Mind, matter and the experimental outlook of John Dewey and Arthur F Bentley*. American Institute for Economic Research: Great Barrington, MA.

Salazar, M. (2013). A humanizing pedagogy: Reinventing the principles and practice of education as a journey toward liberation. *Review of Research in Education*, *37*(1), 121–148.

Simon, Roger, Rosenberg, Sharon, & Eppert, Claudia (Eds.) (2000). *Between hope and despair: Pedagogy and the remembrance of historical trauma*. : Rowman & Littlefield: Lanham, MD.

Weldes, J., & Laffey, M. (2001). Learning to live with U.S. foreign policy and its discontents: The politics of public memory at Kent State, 1970–2001. *School of Sociology, Politics and International Studies* (pp. 08–09). University of Bristol.

3 Sophie Freud

Her name was Sophie Freud. A colleague and friend, she recently passed away at age 97. She spent her youth in Vienna, later earning a BA from Radcliffe, an MSW from Simmons, and a PhD from the Heller School at Brandeis. After a decade of practicing psychiatric social work, she became a professor of social work at the Simmons College School of Social Work. Sophie taught and lectured in Europe and the United States, and developing new courses to teach was her passion. The following offers a brief autobiography:

> On December 5, 1942, readers of *The New Yorker* magazine's "The Talk of the Town" pages were informed that "Sigmund Freud's granddaughter, a pretty girl of eighteen named Sophie, has just arrived in New York" (Robinson & Maloney, 1942, p. 14). Sophie came to the United States along with her mother, Ernestine (Esti) Freud, the wife of Freud's second child and oldest son, Martin. In her newly adopted country, Sophie achieved academic success at Radcliffe College of Harvard University and the Simmons School of Social Work, ultimately earning a Ph.D. from the Florence Heller School of Social Welfare (Brandeis University) in 1970.
>
> (Silverstein, 2008, p. 152)

Both writer and lecturer, Sophie was a clinical social worker, later becoming a professor of clinical social work. She was a true scholar, and through her vocational calling, Sophie used human ideas for building a better world. She survived traumatic early experiences while fleeing her Austrian homeland. I was fascinated by this affable scholar who accepted and supported me. Her family background, scholarship, teaching, learning, and vocational calling were informative and inspirational. Many of our conversations surrounded the mission of the J. J. Jackson Putnam Children's Center, where Sophie worked in the late 1940s and early 1950s:

> I was a student at the Putnam Center in the year 1947/48 and later returned there as a part-time worker, 1958–1963. I came to this country in Nov. 1942 and started Radcliffe College in 1943. My real love has always been books and literature but as a relatively new immigrant I could not concentrate on books., Faithful to my grandfather, clinical social work was the closest I could get to being a psychoanalyst, that is, a psychotherapist without medical training. My main motivation was less in helping folks and more in my interest in hearing stories.
>
> (Sophie Freud, personal communication, January 3, 2018)

We shared a passion for narrative research, collecting and interpreting stories. For Sophie, this began at the J. J. Jackson Children's Center. James Jackson Putnam (1846–1918) was a neurologist and exponent of Sigmund Freud and Freudian analysis. They met in 1909 when, on Freud's only visit to America, he delivered five well-received lectures at Clark University. Putnam, William James, and Freud were colleagues and friends, and their association advanced psychoanalytic theory and work in the United States. Sophie enlightened me as to the theory and practice of psychiatric social work and believed that her best writing was superlative book reviews. Her passion, however, was teaching. Sophie discovered that she had a gift, designing and teaching courses in higher education. In our work, she helped me navigate the nuances of psychoanalytic theory and offered suggestions for my writing and research. One of her letters to Aunt Anna (Anna Freud) describes her return to Putnam:

> [A]nd now a great zest for living. I am working again at the Putnam Children's Center where I worked as a very young mother. I enjoy it much more now, very much as a matter of fact, and I feel very glad that I went back.
>
> (Freud, letter text, Library of Congress)

While not ascribing to a good portion of her famous grandfather's work, Sophie believed there was value in psychoanalytic theory and the "psychoanalytic enterprise." Both intrigued and puzzled by the Method of Currere, she wrote, "Dear Karl, thank you for the lovely photo and the booklet you sent me about *Currere* with your article in it. I read several pieces, trying to understand what it is, including your own, but find it quite difficult to distinguish it from autobiographical and biographical writing, except perhaps a more in-depth examination" (S. Freud, personal communication, February 16, 2019). Fair enough. Currere is difficult to pigeonhole, and I'm continually experimenting with it. At the core, it is autobiographical, but I use it to inform biographical explorations. The work begins with "I" and a personal journey of inquiry. They are not narcissistic endeavors but rather a springboard into curriculum work.

Figure 3.1 Karl Martin and Sophie Freud, Autumn, 2018. (photograph courtesy of the author).

Let me explain. Currere may surface *anywhere* in narrative work. Colleague and friend Sister Margaret Dorgan – a Carmelite nun and scholar - had written theological perspectives regarding prayer and St. Thérèse de Lisieux, and I had the good fortune of meeting with her at a lake house in Ellsworth Maine. At about that time, William Pinar had attended what was described as an "intense encounter" on Catholicism and education. I shared her lecture *Your Personal History as a Narrative of Hope* with Dr. Pinar, where Sister Margaret discusses memory, empathy, and personal history. I suggested that it might dovetail a bit with the method of *currere* and was reminded of Dr. Dwayne Huebner's writing: "To ignore theological language today, however, is to ignore one of the more exciting and viable language communities" (Huebner, 1999, p. 259). In response, Dr. Pinar wrote the following: "Love the photos, Karl, and the formal prose, as well as the yellowed paper. The past is so much more powerful than this paltry (if nightmarish) present. You're kind to send them and kind to send me the lecture. Dovetail indeed. ... Bill" (William Pinar, personal communication, February 4, 2017).

Not so very long ago, Sophie shared her thoughts about the persistence of memory and even Walden Pond.

Sophie: Hi Karl, I just returned home and saw that you called. I had to attend a memorial service.
Karl: I'm sorry. Did you know them well?
Sophie: Not really. He was an acquaintance who passed on, not a close friend, but I'm glad that I went. What have you been doing this afternoon?
Karl: I've just been judging a high school art show through the computer – online, and there are 600 pieces to review, so I am so glad that you called. It's a good time for a break!
Sophie: That sounds like a lot of artwork, but I'm glad I got you on the phone.
Karl: Are you alright with the cold weather? I've heard that the weather near Boston is brutal these past few days.
Sophie: Oh yes, I'm fine, we get used to this weather in Massachusetts. How would you like to do this today? Would you like to talk more on the phone, or do it through emails?
Karl: (I ramble on about unrelated issues.)
Sophie: (She keeps me on topic) Again let me ask the question, would you like to do this through emails or through telephone conversations?
Karl: I would like a little bit of both, a hybrid model, if you will.
  I think that if I supplied you with a couple of questions or something to which you might respond, then I could call, and we can talk about it then.
  What do you think?
Sophie: That's fine, but don't give me too much homework! (Laughing)
  All right then. …What would you like to talk about right now?
Karl: From what I've read you embrace the idea of writing life histories, narratives, and historiographies. You enjoy writing life histories. I've been reading a little bit about the function of memory and tell remembrances might be subjective in unreliable. But let's say that someone lived through the Great San Francisco earthquake, if some facts might be disputed, who better to tell the story than someone who was an eyewitness?
Sophie: Well it's not about your subject that you are writing about – Kent State, but I have published a few books, and my brother and our mother were involved, and it involved traumatic memories. It is entitled *Living in the Shadow of the Freud Family*. We had no coaching, collaboration or dialogue through the process, and yet our accounts are nearly identical. I think that says a lot to the reliability of memory, at least as far as unpleasant memories are concerned.
  If you read it, I hope you find it valuable, but don't know if it would fit the writing you're doing now. That's more about

	psychiatric social work. There are some good historical photographs in the book, however.
Karl:	Are you okay with sending me a couple of photographs from your time at Putnam Children's Center? You did some fascinating work. I'm very much interested in that.
Sophie:	Please give me your address right now, and I'll see what I can find. I would be willing to send you some of the appropriate photographs that you might be able to use in your writing.
	These are beautiful towns, and I have done some teaching at the higher education level at several universities here, including Simmons College. (She pauses, I wait.)
	You know, every summer I swim in the lake that Thoreau has written about.
Karl:	You swim in *Walden Pond?*
Sophie:	Yes, I never miss a summer to swim in that water.
Karl:	Thoreau used to swim in the pond and bring in a little sand to scrub the floors of his cabin.
Sophie:	Yes, he was quite eccentric, and he did build a small place there, right on the lake. My husband and I used to spend some time there in the summers. Karl, who was it that supplied the information that the hero of your story worked at the Putnam Children's Center?
Karl:	Her name was Kathy Cadwell, from British Columbia. She was a genealogist and was very interested in the story. Kathy was 100% certain that she worked there during that time period. (Kathy could research and find most *anything*.)

I didn't endlessly inquire about Sophie's famous grandfather (I *was* fascinated and intrigued, however), and over time, we became friends. At that juncture, I was primarily interested in her contributions to psychiatric social work. Sophie described her journey in the following manner: "[A]nd faithful to my grandfather, clinical social work was the closest I could get to being a psychoanalyst, i.e., a psychotherapist without medical training. My main motivation was less in helping folks and more in my interest in hearing stories" (Sophie Freud, personal communication, January 3, 2018). We both shared an interest in the strong narrative, memoirs, remembrances, and the James J. Jackson Putnam Children's Center, in Boston. This ultimately led to the history of psychoanalysis and Sigmund Freud because of the Center's history. Sophie indicated that her grandfather met Putnam when he delivered his *Five Lectures on Psychoanalysis* in the United States, at Clark University. According to E. Bruce Tucker (1978),

> Impressed by Freud's earnestness and intelligence, Putnam invited him, along with Carl Jung and Sandor Ferenczi, to a retreat in the Adirondacks,

where he plied his visitors with questions. Thus began a friendship which lasted until Putnam's death in 1918 and profoundly affected the reception given to psychoanalysis by the American medical profession.

(p. 528)

Sophie's grandfather or Aunt (Anna Freud, famous for being a psychiatrist who developed theories regarding defense mechanisms) might have recommended she work at the Putnam Center, and I never asked. We had boundaries wordlessly established, and I respected them. When Sophie brought up the topic of psychoanalysis, I leaned in and listened.

Psychoanalysis originated in Austria, but James Jackson Putnam brought the psychoanalytic movement to America. Sigmund Freud was the father of psychoanalysis, and therefore the psychoanalytic component of the *Method of Currere* has European origins, seminal to *currere* thought. Freud represents "the most important and foundational figure in the history of psychoanalysis. In one way or another, all psychoanalysts have been influenced by Freud" (Morris, 2016, p. 320). It's relevant that these psychoanalytic elements (both regressive and progressive) are informed by Sigmund Freud, and his granddaughter's insights are the best place to begin. For example, Sophie recommended Paul Roazen because I was writing about a historical event and also analyzing historical writing about the same subject:

> As a field, history has to be more receptive to psychoanalysis than other of the social sciences: since every narrative has to assume certain conceptions of human nature, and what might be plausible to suppose about motivation, historians have to be sensitive to the existence of psychological systems of thought.
>
> (Roazen, 2001, p. 71)

Roazen wrote about Freud and psychoanalytic theory and believed that history writing was historically valuable. He believed that was the historian's job to sort through facts and decide about relevance, keeping, and discarding.

Following this, evaluations may be made while making sense of things. it is hoped that psychoanalytic theory will be accepted outside of clinical settings.

Sophie was curious about the psychoanalytic component of currere, as were the members of the *Boston Psychiatric Society and Institute*. The Method of Currere was unknown to them, and archivist Olga Umansky took note of their curiosity and enthusiasm. Sophie was enthusiastic about the value of historical and cultural perspectives. Remembering her grandfather's work, she wrote historical narratives and tied them to critical thinking. Roger Simon describes endeavors like this as fundamental to understanding and knowing: "[A]s Freud taught us, learning is not only *about*, but *from* past lives and events (Britzman, 1998).

One of our conversations surrounded a film we had both seen: *Three Identical Strangers*. A documentary with a not-so-transparent message, it follows the lives of identical triplets that were intentionally separated and placed in very differing adoptive homes. Anna Freud had been involved with the research and placement into the new families, occurring in New York City during the 1960s. The research was brought to light when one of the triplets was approached by a young woman upon returning to campus and called a different name. The truth unfolded after a time, and the brothers were reunited. Resentment? Trauma? Yes, there was likely irreparable psychic damage incurred as a result, but for a while, everything seemed fine. They made appearances on television and even began a restaurant called *Three Brothers*.

Regarding the internalization of traumatic experiences, it may not be enough to *tell* the story of past trauma repeatedly. In a sense, the story needs to be *rewritten*. Bessel van der Kolk describes the epiphany of self-discovery through language. He revisits the moment in *The Story of My Life* when Anne Sullivan pours water onto Helen Keller's hand while spelling it on the other: "Water! That word startled my soul, and it awoke, full of the spirit of the morning. Until that day my mind had been like a darkened chamber, waiting for the words to enter and light the lamp, which is thought" (Van Der Kolk, 2014, p. 236). He is aware of the limitations of language and points to the *autobiographical self* that keeps track of time, makes connections, and places them in a coherent story:

> Our narratives change with the telling, as our perspective changes and as we incorporate new input: (Van Der Kolb, p. 238). Dr. Van Der Kolb a more immediate self-awareness, based upon physical sensations. He suggests that persons need to feel safe – without being rushed – and subsequently can find words to communicate that experience as well.
> (p. 238)

If you've done research, you know how it is. A researcher must engender trust, creating a safe place. When my interviewees allowed me enough time to develop a secure relationship, our work was productive. At that point, their defenses (and mine also) were deactivated, and nonlinear explorations through currere thought could emerge.

Two forms of self-awareness – the emotional and the narrative part of the brain act in concert, cooperating with each other. I believe that the Method of Currere is at work in my biographical explorations, but research must employ ethical practice, and this requires intuition. A few years ago – on a road trip to interview Sophie – my wife Michelle suggested I look for a "sign." A minute later, a truck passed, a message emblazoned on the

Figure 3.2 Interstate 84, Eastern Pennsylvania. (photo courtesy of Karl W. Martin).

back: *Be Kind, Be Careful, Be Yourself*. I was reminded again of the writing of William Pinar: "The student of educational experience accepts that at any given moment she or he is located in history and culture, always in a singularly meaningful way, a situation to be expressed autobiographically (if indirectly) through the curriculum" (Pinar, 2012, p. 45). What better counsel than the phrase emblazoned on the back of that semi? It was a reminder to practice ethics while remaining true to my vision" (Martin, 2022, p. 31). The ethical components are best described as follows: "The modes may include dialogue in the spoken and written and visual to affect their aims to adhere to the principles of respect, beneficence, nonmaleficence, and justice in a way that is mutually beneficial to the participant and the researcher" (Aluwihare-Samaranayake, 2012, p. 64).

Trauma

Sophie Freud believed that an outstanding finding in her research was the confirmation of the paramount importance of parental attitudes for the adjustment of the child. Affection and acceptance by *both* parents were necessary for the treatment of neuroses. This worked in tandem with the "psychoanalytic enterprise" (her terminology) to address trauma and its effects.

Sigmund Freud had to flee his native homeland like his daughter and granddaughter, later writing a reinterpretation of Moses's flight from Egypt and rebirth of the faith. Literary critic Cathy Caruth wrote about historical construction and trauma, where she suggests "a delayed constitution of historical understanding due to the specific, not immediately perceived impact of traumatic events" (Friedlander, 1992, p. 43). Following this, early ideological stances of this disruptive – if not catastrophic – tragedy at Kent State may resist redemptive interpretation. There wasn't an adequate resolution 50 years after May 4, and there may not be one in the future. Friedlander points to differing traumas: "If we consider both German and Jewish contemporaries of the Nazi period – contemporary adults, adolescents or children, even the children of these groups – what was traumatic for the one group was obviously not traumatic for the other" (Friedlander, 1992, p. 45). During the clashes students of my age had with the older generation, it seemed that we were fighting fascism itself. To me, there was – and is – denial or ambivalence expressed by those who supported the National Guard, and perhaps even the guardsmen themselves. Do we even believe that there may be a collective sense of guilt regarding authority figures and the guard? Not likely. If the United States can't revisit troubling histories of genocide and slavery, how will it ever revisit May 4, if at all?

In the case of psychoanalytic thought, history writing through the method of currere is perfectly acceptable: "The principles that historians invoke to make the past meaningful are often moral, ethical and political, if not down-right intuitive and capable of being fully justified" (Roazen, 2001, p. 74). There is room for more than one history because history itself is a form of literature. Like so many inventions, psychoanalysis can be traced back to Sigmund Freud. Just like Edison invented the first vacuum tube and light bulb, Freud developed a phenomenon that stubbornly refuses to go away almost a century after the fact. Curriculum studies applications exist that are informed by psychoanalytic theory. One of these is William Pinar's *Method of Currere*.

References

Aluwihare-Samaranayake, D. (2012). Ethics in qualitative research: A view of the participants' and researchers' world from a critical standpoint. *International Journal of Qualitative Methods*, *11*(2), 64–81.

Friedlander, S. (1992). Trauma, transference and "working through" in writing the history of the "Shoah". *History and Memory*, *4*(1), 39–59.

Freud, S. (1989). *Inhibitions, symptoms and anxiety*. J. Strachey (Ed.) W. W. Norton & Company: New York, NY.

Freud, S. (2002). *American Journal of Psychotherapy*, 438–440.

Huebner, D. E. (1999) *The lure of the transcendent: Collected essays*. (Ed. Vikki Hillis. Collected and introduced by William F. Pinar.). Lawrence Erlbaum: Mahwah, N.J.

Library of Congress. Letters from Sophie Freud to Anna Freud.

Martin, K. (2022). Finding Marya: The road east. *Currere Exchange Journal*, 6(2), 27–42.

Morris, M. (2016). Psychoanalytic curriculum concepts. *Counterpoints*, 499(2), 319–372.

Roazen, P. (2001). What is a fact? Eva Rosenfeld and Historiography. *Journal of Religion and Health*, 40(1), 71–78.

Silverstein, B. (2008). Living in the shadow of the Freud family (review). *American Imago*, 65(1, 152–160.

Tucker, E. B. (1978). James Jackson Putnam: An American perspective on the social uses of psychoanalysis, 1895–1918. *The New England Quarterly*, 51(4), 527–546.

4 Patricia Gless

Patricia was a nursing student at that time, attending class on May 4. Glenn Frank burst into the classroom and suggested that there "could be trouble," imploring them to get off campus. She gathered up her things, left campus immediately, and drove home to Ravenna. At that time, she joined her mother at Robinson Memorial Hospital after learning that wounded students would be arriving. Her mother was the nursing supervisor there, in charge of staffing and admissions. She was given the unenviable task of notifying the parents of the slain and escorting them to the room where their children were taken. Her mother never discussed the subject again, not with anyone. It's possible that persons from her

Figure 4.1 People ducking and running for cover in and around a parking lot (*Kent State University Libraries. Special Collections and Archives*, May 4, 1970. Kent State University. News Service).

generation didn't require as much reflection or discussion. She just wanted to forget, to move on, or perhaps she intentionally repressed the memories: "Any kind of a substitute memory is a constant sign – even though only perhaps only a characteristic and revealing sign – of tendentious forgetfulness which is motivated by repression" (Freud, 1960, p. 24).

In her own words: "My response to being asked to leave campus was just that…I left campus and got a ride back to my home in Ravenna where later that afternoon I was called in to work at Robinson Memorial Hospital where I worked as a student nurse and helped to care for the injured students."

As they arrived on gurneys, Pat assisted with triage of the incoming wounded. It was a deliberate, focused endeavor. Pat felt as if she was assisting and treating battle or disaster victims to maximize the number of survivors. She was.

Reference

Freud, S. (1960). Translated James Strachey. *The psychopathology of everyday life*. W. W. Norton & Company.

5 Jerry M. Lewis, Professor Emeritus

Jerry was the father of two of my students when I arrived in Kent. He and his family lived down the block, on Akron Boulevard, a half-mile-long strip of identical duplexes. Known to have the "best backyards" in Kent, his son Damon and friends would routinely knock on my door to play football, offering me the position of full-time quarterback. Jerry was involved with the parent-teacher organization and a supporter of the arts. He was a faculty marshal on May 4, standing in the parking lot when gunfire sprayed the asphalt. He instinctively dove for whatever cover he could find, and when the shooting stopped, the body of Sandra Scheuer was 10 feet away. His descriptions of the students, National Guard, and shootings are the recollections of a well-disciplined mind. Professor Lewis had military experience, which resulted in a reflexive, disciplined response to danger and to the shootings. Therefore, he didn't experience the same feelings of helplessness as the much younger students. He had been in combat and immediately realized that the guardsmen were using live ammunition.

We talked for a while about our parent-teacher relationships at Longcoy School and living on the west side of Kent. Akron Boulevard is a straight road with identical duplexes, each driveway serving four families. Jerry described them as having "the best backyards in Kent," and that is a fair assessment. I reminded Jerry about a long football pass I threw to his son Damon, and he reminded me that I was the Longcoy Olympic Games leader, in 1976. Jerry said that I carried the torch and led the parade. Interestingly, I remembered little of the Longcoy School Olympics of 1976. After our connection and exchange of pleasantries, Jerry signaled that he was ready to begin. Initially, Jerry wanted to talk without interruption:

DOI: 10.4324/9781003399094-5

Figure 5.1 Professor Jerry M. Lewis at a book signing. (photo courtesy of Professor Jerry M. Lewis).

We all wore a marshaling blue armband that Glenn Frank had provided
The guardsmen had surrounded the Commons.
I stood at the corner of Taylor Hall.
I saw a few local cops. Norm Duffy was a KSU cop, and he was there.
There were army jeeps, Kent Policeman and regular Kent State University cops.
Three guardsmen and a cop in an army jeep drove up to some of the students.:
The cop said, "Go home," which was confusing to the students because "home" was Ashtabula or Painesville. "Home" might also be the dormitory where they lived.
The students were chanting anti-war slogans at the victory bell.
So, I thought. ...Let's go down and talk to the students.
Then the situation changed...

"Here they come!" Guardsmen were marching past the burned-out ROTC Building. They began shooting tear gas. Tear gas shot with canisters had a cheap perfume smell and then you teared up. Rubbing your eyes makes it worse. I don't know why, but I went past the Pagoda and headed down

into the parking lot. When I got halfway down, I looked over where Centennial Hall is now. At some distance, I thought I saw a student laying on the ground, so I thought I should see what's going on with him. He was a blind student who had been teargassed and was on the ground.
I went past the tennis courts and gave him first aid. I told him not to rub his eyes. This was on the path that led to Tri-Towers. I felt like I wanted to get back to the Prentice Hall parking lot... I just felt like I should get back to that parking lot. I don't know why, but I did. So, I walked back to the edge of the parking lot, and just as I did...

> The guard were heading up the hill when I got back.
> You probably remember that famous picture of guard kneeling, aiming at Alan...
> Anyway, when the guard went up the hill. ...When they got to the Pagoda...
> When they got to the Pagoda there were 76 guardsmen there, and total of 28 fired their weapons.
> The right rear echelon turned over 130 degrees and fired their weapons.
> Smoke came from the barrels – so I knew that real rounds were fired from being in the army
> So, I dove to the right and that took me out of the line of fire.
> I saw the guard turning, saw left-handed Sgt. Myron Pryor extend his gun.
> Over the years, I've learned to tell myself a story so I can remember what happened, what details.
> I remember saying out loud to myself, or at least thinking that I needed "to tell myself a story" to help myself remember. I remember saying, "At least nobody got stuck," meaning bayonetted by the guard.
> Just as I thought or said that, the right rear echelon turned and fired.
> I saw them turn in unison.
> Some fired into the air or the ground.
> Some didn't fire at all.
> I dove for cover. When I came up, I took six or seven steps towards the parking lot
> Some students said, "Dr. Lewis, those are blanks." I realized that many of the students thought they were firing blanks.
> There was a different perspective - a legitimacy about having a PhD in those days. I called out to them and said, "Please leave now," and they did.
> Sandra Scheuer was lying on the ground near me.
> There was a wounded student down on the road behind me.

Sandra, myself, and a male wounded student were near to each other. I was standing near two students, and I pulled them to me when I saw a gurney coming with a student on it, which turned out to be Allison Krause who was taken away on that gurney. "You don't want to see this." One of them thanked me about six months later.

Again...and I can't stress this enough...I clearly saw the guard turning, in unison.

In the aftermath...an RA from Prentice Hall asked me to go on the loudspeaker and announce something. I went on and said a few things.

What's interesting was that the students were all sitting down. That never happened at rallies, and it was the first time I had ever seen that. I was the junior marshal, following Glenn's lead. Glenn Frank got the students to do this, to sit down, and convinced them to leave. The students slowly got up and started slowly moving out, headed towards the tennis courts and disappeared. Meanwhile, we had been negotiating with General Canterbury to let the students stay on the Common. He was in a business suit and gas mask when the guardsmen fired on the students, and he knew exactly what happened. He said...He told us..."If they don't leave...We're going to come again if they don't leave in five minutes."

Oh yeah. And they were at port arms. You could see them forming up. At this point, you're just reacting. You usually get scared after the fact – but that's when I was really scared...at that time...when I saw the guard getting ready to come again. Port arms I remember well from being in the army. The rifle is held diagonally in front of the body with the muzzle pointing upward to the left. They were going to come again. The guard was coming again to engage and fire upon more students if they didn't disperse. Glenn said that "[i]t would be a bloodbath," and he wasn't kidding. He wasn't exaggerating. The documentation was based upon a policeman saying he smelled gunpowder. All the rounds that the National Guard fired. The Guard fired between 61 and 67 rounds." The original count was 61, but further research has the count at 67. Howard Means' book is a good book about the shootings, published two years ago. After spending time with several reporters, one who was one of my students, I began to realize the scope of May 4. It wasn't until the Scranton Commission about the symbolic power of May 4 during August of 1970 that the importance of that day was a cultural event.

You see...it dawned on me then, two months later. Initially, I was micro-focused, worried about finishing classes, "polishing" my dissertation (which I never did), and tenure. I was worried about my calling, my teaching, and called my Dean, the Provost. I asked him if I should publish an article in a left-oriented journal, and he replied "Sure! Why not?"

I wasn't that analytical in retrospect, but I thought…I tried to…I didn't know the answers, but tried to figure things out…

We were all exiting to the right by the tennis courts. A guy with a denim jacket with an upside-down flag was cursing, shouting. I told him to "[b]e quiet! We have women in the crowd!" It seems ridiculous now, but you see…when you're in a crisis situation, you don't always say or do things that are rational. You just *try* and keep calm and help. It wasn't until I got home on Akron Boulevard that I realized I could also have been killed. But I really didn't realize it until I talked with a reporter from the *Beacon Journal*.

Jerry has identified four decisions made by the National Guardsmen that – while not defending their presence on campus with the accompanying bloodshed, offer acknowledgment of good judgment by some of the troops. We're to incorporate this into a curriculum for elementary students to offer a fair perspective.

1 The first decision – and it's vital to point out – in the absence of clear leadership, the guardsmen had to decide whether to fire their weapons or not.
2 Then, you have two categories. The people who *didn't* fire their weapons had to be careful of the soldiers who fired their weapons. In fact, Major Harry Jones was rather heroic because he came down the line hitting their guns. That's the second decision, to get out of the way.
3 The third decision was made by the guardsmen who decided to fire.
4 The fourth decision is what direction they fired, whether to fire into the air, into the ground, or into the crowd.

Karl: Have you fired an M1? You were in the army, correct?
Jerry: Yes. I was a qualified sharpshooter. I was scared of the M1 at first because I'd never fired anything but a BB rifle at Boy Scout camp. The M1 is powerful, accurate, and controllable. The Germans thought when they introduced the M1 that every American had a machine gun. It has an eight-round clip and is considered a semi-automatic weapon. My expertise was in the 250-yard range. The guardsmen here were much closer. That's one thing the army did a very good job of, teaching you how to fire an M1.

In addition, as both a sociology professor and scholar, Jerry offers both autobiographical and societal perspectives based upon his experiences. He has contributed extensive and seminal research surrounding May 4, 1970, using biographical and autobiographical text and insights. "Autobiography becomes a medium for both teaching and research because each entry expresses the particular peace its author has made between the individuality

48   Jerry M. Lewis, Professor Emeritus

Figure 5.2 Pictured are guardsmen deployed on campus adjacent to West Main Street. Behind the Jeep is the main campus pictured with Hilltop Drive. Kent, Merrill, and University Hall are seen in the background (photo courtesy of Paul Gailey, May 3, 1970).

of his or her subjectivity and the intersubjective and public character of meaning" (Pinar, Reynolds, Slattery, & Taubman, 1995, p. 324).

Jerry's scholarship and research contribute greatly to keeping the history of May 4th accurate and intact. He crafted an excellent manual for teaching May 4 for the 40th anniversary, beginning with a dedication to Jeffrey Miller, Allison Krause, William Schroeder, and Sandra Scheuer. It is designed for teachers who want to include elements of May 4 in their coursework. He opens with a physical description of the university and surrounding countryside, then launches into an empirical look at the events of May 4, 1970.

He directs teachers to provide accurate information and the resources available, whether books, video, or archival materials. Jerry recommends interdisciplinary analytical strategies while encouraging student expression through speaking and writing. His goal is to engender "lifelong learning," an element of a liberal education. Jerry's scholarship ensures that the teaching and learning about May 4 engenders critical thinking.

Reference

Pinar, W. F., Reynolds, W. M., Slattery, P., & Taubman, P. M. (1995). (17) Curriculum as autobiographical/biographical text. *Counterpoints: Understanding Curriculum: An Introduction to the Study of Historical and Contemporary Curriculum Discourses* (pp. 516–566). Peter Lang: New York.

6 Alan Canfora, Lifelong Activist

Alan didn't mind that I use a recording device. Our time together took place in a noisy downtown Akron restaurant, conversational and relaxed. Alan was affable, putting me instantly at ease. I've come to understand that he was like that with most people.

It forced me to really listen. I think if there's anything worth retaining, a researcher ought to be able to remember it, and that's how our time unfolded. I often didn't want an iPhone or recorder to come between us and create an impediment. Something I noticed in Alan – and I didn't know him before – is how he represented his age. Alan was continuing his mission, his vocational calling to keep May 4 in our collective memory. I wondered if learning more about May 4th would live up to my expectations. For decades I had considered the idea of writing about May 4, 1970. Alan didn't disappoint. That feeling never wears off, that excitement each person creates while telling their story.

When Alan conducted a tour, there was an added dimension. The setting, on-site, with rain and mist added an intimacy to the experience. Umbrellas brandished, fog surrounding us, we all moved closer to one another. Alan talked tirelessly while standing in front of Taylor Hall as we looked down on the Commons. Standing in front of that impressive building, its features are imprinted in the brain. The entire site is virtually unchanged. You imagine its true form, relieved of the burdensome new gym, no longer compelled to see that alien structure. Even though I had walked this area hundreds of times, Alan's enthusiasm and expertise rendered me as much a tourist as the other charges. When he spoke, I could picture the massive smokestacks, and where the new gym sits, I saw open fields. We had left 2019 and entered 1970, if only for a few minutes, journeying five decades back in time. I had become jaded, but with Alan, I was engulfed with awe.

Alan was shot through the wrist on May 4, finding refuge behind a tree when the fusillade began. The photograph of him waving a black flag at the National Guard is legendary, and his life's work had been to keep the historical events and memory of the shootings alive. Becoming a teacher (or practitioner, instructor, and curriculum leader) requires an almost

DOI: 10.4324/9781003399094-6

Figure 6.1 John Darnell closely followed and photographed the National Guard as they advanced on the Commons toward the pagoda. (photograph courtesy of John Darnell, May 4, 1970).

missional calling, and Alan embodied this. His work illuminated the intrinsic drive that "unconsciously, from the motivation of his occupation, reaches out for all relevant information, and holds to it. The vocation acts as both magnet to attract, and as glue to hold" (Dewey, 1915/2009, p. 297).

This might explain why leaders like Alan would want to examine what initially influenced, motivated, and pointed them toward their vocational calling. A historical biographical narrative is a worthy means to tell this story, "an education which acknowledges the full intellectual and social meaning of a vocation would include instruction in the historical background of present conditions" (Dewey, 1915/2009, p. 306). Alan understood all of this and epitomized what an activist embodies at all stages of his life. That is what I meant by "age," the seasons of his life and work evolving with age and experience. While I didn't personally know the younger Alan, it was easy to see that married life and fatherhood were good for him. He said so himself. Alan continued his work and was writing his memoirs, adamant that his work point to gaps in the knowledge and reveal the facts about a signal to fire.

Alan was not one to allow himself to become isolated or lose his commitment. He *lived* his vocational calling, refusing to retreat into the path of least resistance. Alan was generous in sharing his insights, and I immensely enjoyed our conversations. We did more than talk. The exchanges became what William Pinar has labeled "complicated conversations." According to William Pinar, "conversations are complicated because people are talking to each other. And because teachers talk not only to their students but also to their own mentors, their own experiences and their contents, because the contents themselves are conversations (...) The conversation is complicated because it happens between everyone in society" (Süssekind, 2014, p. 207).

Our conversations could be defined as a form of *collaborative lead-learning*. Identified, conceived, and developed by James G. Henderson, this manner of inquiry aims "to encourage professional educators to engage in a lead-learning, collegial reflective inquiry approach to curriculum development. Such an approach is informed by both curriculum and collaborative inquiry by all participants involved and designed to be a constructive alternative to Tyler's (1949) rationale" (Henderson, 2016, p. 127). My colleague Jennifer Lowers and I interpreted this process as follows:

Lead-learning that takes place among two or more lead learners
Lead learners do not merely share resources but add to them in some way in order to create a unique learning experience.
Helpful for understanding complex concepts and terminology pertaining to curriculum work.

Provides lead learners with the opportunity to practice explaining complicated curriculum concepts and terminology to colleagues who are unfamiliar with them.
This can take many forms, such as peer review, deliberative and/or complicated conversations, advice/recommendations, clarification, drawing, music, activities, brainstorming, e-mails, text messages – all while comparing personal experiences and perspectives.
The benefits of these exchanges are as follows:

Lead-learning that takes place among two or more lead learners can provide curriculum workers with the opportunity to be introduced to new ideas.
Lead learners are intrinsically motivated.
Collaborative lead-learning is highly conducive of capacity building.
Lead-learning gives you the opportunity to learn from others and to be exposed to new information.
This allows us to make connections among the work of writers to whom we are introduced and those with whom we are already familiar.
Lead-learning opens your mind to the connections that exist in our universe.

This describes well my work with Alan. He was interdisciplinary in thinking, but his true field was activism and dissent as applied to Kent State University. He was widely regarded as an authority on the subject: "Mr. Canfora went on to become a walking encyclopedia on all aspects of 'Kent State,' the university's name becoming synonymous with the shootings and with state-sanctioned violence – so much so that in 1986 the university tried to rebrand itself as 'Kent.' Mr. Canfora spent the rest of his life making sure the university would never erase May 4 from its history" (K. Q. Seelye, *New York Times*, January 17, 2021). If we consider history to be qualified as collective memory, Alan had discovered his true calling to keep this memory viable, his vocation a call to action and service following the tragedy of May 4, 1970: "An occupation is the only thing which balances the distinctive capacity of an individual with his social service. To find out what one is fitted to do and to secure an opportunity to do it is the key to happiness" (Dewey, 1915/2009 p. 376).

I asked him how he could trust his memory. Might he have altered some of the facts through telling and retelling. Alan replied that he continually "sharpened" the memory of the events of May 4, mindful of the need for accuracy by keeping *every* detail at the forefront. Nothing was condensed into generalities: "Normal forgetting takes place by way of condensation. In this way it becomes the basis for the formation of concepts. What is isolated is perceived clearly. Repression makes use of the mechanism of condensation and produces a confusion with other similar cases. – In addition, trends from other quarters take possession of the indifferent material and cause it to be distorted or falsified" (Freud, 1960, p. 176). I believe that the knowledge Alan shared was both *factually* and *spiritually* true. He had managed his trauma by telling and retelling his story. He *believed* in keeping alive the memory of May 4 and never contradicted himself. Perhaps it helped him personally process the trauma. I believe what he said was true. To sum up, Alan "walked his talk" in a unique and committed way.

I watched Alan's hands as he spoke, because they were always in motion, expressive and gesturing. Occasionally he would make a small sketch on a napkin of Taylor Hall and the parking lot, and I wish I had kept one of them. I paid attention, trying to understand his memory of what happened there. He believed that the "Move the Gym" activism marked the end of gathered resistance but also brought renewed attention to the history at Kent State.

Alan lived by principle, with tenacious enthusiasm to match. He was determined, driven, generous, and affable. I believe that's why he agreed to talk with me. After his experiences, I wondered how marriage and fatherhood changed him. I didn't know Alan previously, but it seemed as if there was harmony in his life.

Alan Canfora, Lifelong Activist 53

Figure 6.2 Alan beginning a tour – on-site and in his element. (photo courtesy of the author).

We connected in other ways. Alan once said, "I'm hoping we maybe are developing a friendship That's where I thought this was going." I agreed. We were both guitar players, both had Fender Telecasters, and grew up with the same music. The COVID-19 pandemic changed everything. People became islands, even avoiding friends and family. Alan texted me after a couple of months, just before May 4: "I'm laying low, trying to stay healthy, and I hope you are also" (Alana Canfora, personal communication May 2, 2020). On that day – my birthday – my wife and I ate pizza on a bench in Hudson. Police drones flew up the street, surveilling people to enforce social distancing, a memory disturbing to this day. Before things improved, Alan passed away. Our final communication was on May 4, a 50th-anniversary virtual commemoration. I texted some early morning photos while jogging past the empty site, and he liked the images a lot.

Key Points from Alan's Tour

People will learn these lessons into the future…other universities, other politicians, other governments. We will not repeat what happened here on May 4, 1970. (Alan holds up a photo of himself, waving a black flag). This is a picture of a long-haired bold young man, daring to stand while at least three guardsmen are aiming in his direction. This was me, at age 21.

About 200 students gathered down there (points to Victory Bell) to protest Richard Nixon's announcement the night before on April 30, the invasion of Cambodia; the expansion of the war from Vietnam into another country, Cambodia. That was very controversial. Not just here at Kent State, but around the country, students went out that evening on Thursday night, April 30, and the next day on Friday, May 1.

And they protested all across the country. But only here at Kent State would culminate – four days later – during that weekend – the protest with a very historic and controversial massacre, which triggered the *only* national student strike in American history. Over four million students went out on strike, protesting what happened here, vigorously at their colleges and universities from coast to coast. It had never happened before. It has never happened since – a national student strike. It was provoked, and I hope you understand this...by then President Richard Nixon. He expanded the war from Vietnam into another country.

Allison Krause was in Engelmann Hall that morning, walking to look for her boyfriend, who lived in Johnson (Hall). Barry was waiting up on the hill here. You can see Allison in the photograph. I was there with my black flags. I made those flags that morning – out of black material – as symbols of our anger of our despair. Having attended a funeral only 10 days earlier of a guy killed in Vietnam.

This tree saved my life. And now it's saving us from the rain. (Alan places his hand on the tree) I love this tree. There were about 32 more trees on that beautiful hill, which was called Blanket Hill. And the reason it was called Blanket Hill was because back during the 1950s – because of rock and roll and Elvis, it corrupted our youth because students would come up here and make out at night. That was mainly because the dorm visitation rules were so conservative. Guys weren't allowed to go into girls' college rooms. It was even worse at other colleges.

(Alan again shows the photograph of the guard kneeling and aiming). This group that was kneeling, they're aiming at me in that picture, which I think maybe most of you would see now. Those are the guys who did the killing when they marched back up the hill and fire down this way.

So...at the point when they were out there. The truth is those are the guys with their fingers on the triggers. They're picking out their targets. That's what I've always said is, and I really do believe this.

Until they marched out of there at 12:10 p.m., 12:15 p.m. ...They came marching back up this grade on 12:20 and they fired the weapons at 12:24 p.m. I believe the best way to summarize what happened on that day, those 24 minutes, was a "humping" mission. Troop G was seeking out their targets, seeing who's waving the black flag. Who was throwing rocks? Well, Jeff Miller, Alison Krauss, and Dean Kaylor threw a rock or two.

When they shot the guns, Dean Kahler was paralyzed for life. Dean had thrown a rock. He'd never been to a demonstration in his whole life. But he got so upset by the guardsmen chasing him...and the tear gas. He threw a rock just through frustration.

The troop off to the left, they didn't kill anybody. On the right are about a dozen guys, looking over their shoulders, the whole way up the hill. I say they were picking out targets, but of course, when they testified at the Cleveland Federal Court in 1975, they said, "Oh, we were looking out for rocks."

Nobody was throwing any rocks as they were going up the hill. But that's the situation. They were looking for people to shoot. Now I am really against conspiracy theories, but there's reason to believe that Troop G had a plan in their minds. When they got to that hilltop, there was going to be an order to fire. And that's what happened. There was a verbal command and about a dozen men simultaneously fired, and I saw this. Think of the odds of this happening if any of you are mathematics majors. What is the probability that a dozen soldiers would March up the hill and suddenly, *simultaneously*...12 guys stop together, turn together, raise their weapons together, start to shoot, and continue to shoot. *Simultaneously*. For 12.53 seconds? Very unlikely.

How would that happen without a command to fire? The guardsmen later filled out their own reports in their own handwriting.

Not so long ago I happened to be conducting research at Yale University's library archive with a Vietnam veteran by the name of Robert Johnson, from Brooklyn, New York. He was obsessed about Kent State, and I pay tribute where it's deserved. He would come here and see those spaces marked off in the parking lot from 1970 and was determined to find out how it was allowed to happen.

They turned and fired. They wounded only four of us on the hillside. Joe Lewis by that sidewalk. John Cleary by the metal sculpture. Joe Lewis was shot in the stomach and the ankle, John Cleary in the middle of his chest...went in and out. He fell on the ground and *Life* magazine ran a picture with him on the cover, right there by the metal sculpture.

I was down here by this tree, shot through the wrist. Tom Grace was out in the open. A bullet went in at the top of his ankle and blew the bottom of his foot off. He walks with an insert to this day.

It's important to ask why the guardsmen felt so threatened. They fired down the hillside, which only had 18 students on it. Photographic analysis has *proven* there were only 18 students on the hillside. The vast majority were in that parking lot. That's where the most radical students were gathered.

Reference

Dewey, J. (1915/2009). *Democracy and education*. The Macmillan Company: New York.
Freud, S. (1960). Translated James Strachey. *The psychopathology of everyday life*. W. W. Norton & Company.
Castner, D. J., Gornik, R. G., Henderson, J. G., & Samford, W. L.
Henderson, J. G. (2016).
Seelye, K. Q. *The New York Times*, January 17, 2021.
Süssekind, M. L. (2014). *Quem é William F. Pinar? [Who is William F. Pinar?]* DP et Alii: Petrópolis.

7 Lynn Csernotta Beaton, Artist and Teacher

I met Lynn on a walking tour given by Alan Canfora. She and her sister listened to his descriptions and commentary with rapt attention, having more than a passing interest. Lynn was there – on-site – watching from 30 yards away when the guard turned and fired. She saw and heard *everything*. Her account of the demonstration, activists, National Guard, shootings, and aftermath were raw, vivid, and graphic. At the time she was a sophomore art student, and most of her reflections are included. Lynn provides relevant details, commentary, and genuine compassion. In addition, Lynn shared something that many cannot. She had been an art student – later an artist and art teacher. She had the ability to see things as they were then – and now, in the present day. Lynn had a special way of looking at those events, something that might be called the eye of an artist. Elliot Eisner (1992) describes and explains what this entails:

> The artist's eye finds delight and significance in the suggestive subtlety of the remembrances and places of our existence. The work of art displays these insights, makes them vivid, and reawakens our awareness of what we have learned not to see. Thus, art is the alchemy of the humdrum, the moral one. It serves to help us rediscover meaning in the world of vision, it provides for the development of sensibility, it serves as an image of what life may be.
>
> (Eisner, 1992, p. 16)

Regrettably, Lynn recently has passed away, but I was fortunate to work with her and call her a friend. Lynn was compassionate and genuine, and said that the events of May 4 weighed heavily on her throughout life. I enjoyed her continuing biographical updates, which were sprinkled throughout our many texts and conversations. It was a gradual process that led up to a formal interview at her home, a "step-by-step" unfolding. From Pinar: "The blind spot notion has to do with my experience of biographic and intellectual movements as steps. There is always a next step, although it may be veiled. It's as if it is a dark spot to be illumined, and

Figure 7.1 Lynn Csernotta Beaton. (photograph courtesy of her sister, Nancy Csernotta Joyce).

once illumined, the step may be taken" (1978, p. 112). Pinar's "next step" was the formulation of a method a few years after the shootings, part of the "Reconceptualization" of curriculum studies.

Lynn and I shared our personal experiences through an informal *currere* exploration. It was gradual, illuminating those many "dark spots" that "reveal the ways that histories (both collective and individual) and hope suffuse our moments, and to study them through telling our stories of educational experience" (Grumet, 1981, p. 118). As to the latent and manifest meaning, Lynn passed away before we could delve into further analysis and synthesis. She was at first hesitant to share her experiences, wanting to hold them close to her, but Lynn eventually wanted to talk. We both were artists, and we began with our art experiences and endeavors – a common ground. Eventually, Lynn was willing to talk about May 4. She was unfamiliar with currere but appreciated the idea of a currere journey.

The regressive and progressive elements of currere are not therapy, but I was fortunate to be present when she was ready to talk – in familiar surroundings, in a comfortable kitchen, coffee in hand, with a friendly dog roaming about.

I was greatly saddened by her passing. I am left to write the *currere* of persons no longer able to undertake the steps themselves. I write about Lynn to honor her story and the person she was. Lynn and I both believed that the practice of art is a psychological activity (Jung, 1978, p. 65) and can be approached from a psychological angle as deriving from "psychic motives." This is how we met:

A Kent State tour was to be provided by Alan Canfora, and I arrived at the May 4 Visitor's Center to speak with him before it started.
Alan walked over to shake my hand.

AC: I'm so glad you were able to make it! It's not the best day weather-wise, but we should be fine.
KM: Alan, I'm so glad to be here, and thanks for the invitation.
 (The group began to gather, and the atmosphere was heavy, fog rolling in. It started to rain as Alan began the tour)
AC: We'll begin here. Please gather around everyone! Toward the tour's end, we were all standing in the parking lot at Prentice Hall after he talked about each student who had fallen.
AC: How familiar is everyone with this place? Was anyone on campus then?
LB: I was on campus.
AC: Where were you on campus?
LB: I was right here! Here…when the shootings happened. Right here!
AC: Really? Well, I hope I can hear your story.

The women were Lynn Csernotta Beaton and her sister. They listened to his descriptions and commentary with rapt attention and had more than a passing interest. I approached them after Alan concluded the tour:

KM: My name is Karl, and I'm writing about May 4. Would you mind meeting up for an interview sometime?
 Lynn agreed, and we exchanged numbers, indicating that email wasn't always reliable for contacting her. Lynn was always involved and engaged with family, especially her many grandchildren, and extremely invested in her dog's many health issues. As a result, we talked or texted for two years before meeting for an interview.

November 4, 2021

Lynn invited me into her home, and we moved from the entryway through the living room and into the kitchen. There was a breakfast island, and she thoughtfully brewed two cups of coffee. An affectionate golden retriever ambled into the room, putting a warm nose in my hand.

I was ready to jump back in time and was not disappointed. She guided me through things like a time-travel tourist. One can read about the shootings and tour the site, but it can seem abstract, unreal. While Lynn shared her story, I could almost hear the gunfire and smell the smoke. The National Guardsmen deployed were carrying live ammunition that day. Many of the students thought they were firing blanks, but for the four dead lying in the parking lot, it had been a very real event.

Lynn Csernotta Beaton, Artist and Teacher   59

This is Karl Martin, interviewing Lynn Csernotta Beaton regarding her experiences on May 4, 1970. The date was November 5, 2021, and what follows is the transcript of our interview:

Karl: On that morning I was a freshman 60 miles away – at Westminster College – but it was sunny, and it was a crisp start to the day. Would you please begin with that morning?

Lynn: Yes. It was deceivingly crisp. It looked like it was going to be warm. But it was clear and cool then.

I was walking where we lived – I was married and lived in Silver Oaks Apartments.

I knew there was going to be a protest at the bell by Blanket Hill. I knew that was happening.

Umm…I showed glass slides at Art History class at 12:00…so…

I was walking from Silver Oaks over to where I showed the slides, which is right across from Blanket Hill in one of those old buildings.

When I got there – of course – the protests were already going on…

When I reached the Commons, the kids were assembled around the Victory Bell,

with the chanting that everyone knows:

"One Two Three Four! We don't want your fucking war!"

We hated what was happening,

and kids were reading there around the bell, burying a copy of the Constitution there…

But the greater group of kids were actually lined up on the sidewalk, like…watching what was going on…

And as I walked down the sidewalk past the bell, and I saw the National Guard troops on the other side of Blanket Hill

And…of course, I had to stop too, because…

the National Guard started yelling.

Disperse! Disperse! We order you to disperse!

And everybody was just standing there watching them…

You know, like…*Really*?

What are they doing there with their guns and their bayonets and their army trucks on campus?

At the time, it didn't feel that threatening.

Even when it got to the point where they started throwing tear gas at the students,

it still didn't feel that threatening.

And I know you know what happened, with the tear gas…

The kids picked them up and started throwing it back at them.

Which really ticked them off., needless to say.

So…the next thing you know…

No one was moving...
Can you imagine? The guard was there with their Jeeps and weapons...their bayonets and their army trucks.
We belonged there. *They didn't belong there!*
We were all thinking...*What are you doing on campus?*
The next thing you know, when no one was moving they started coming. ... They started to come at us with their bayonets and their guns.
They didn't really target the protesters.
They just started to sweep everyone up the hill. When all the students were standing there watching.
There was no escape.

KM: Towards the pagoda? Towards Taylor Hall?

LB: Yeah. At the time, it was the architecture building.
(The architecture building, which also housed the Department of Journalism.)

LB: I was by myself at that point, then when I got up there, I ran into two friends...and we started talking. I was talking to them and...
This part I'm a little confused about, you know. They came up...the fact that part of the guard came up from the football field. That other group of National Guard people came up from the football practice field.
(This was Company C, with Myron Pryor.)
Later, they said we were throwing rocks.
They talked about us throwing rocks
How many rocks are on campus where they mow the grass?
Is that going to make sense?
Unless people brought rocks. I mean, there weren't rocks there to throw at anyone.
I didn't see anybody doing that.
Not that it couldn't have happened.
They walked past where I was.
They walked past where I was standing.
Turned around and started firing.
I mean, it's still in my brain.
Da! Da Da Da Da Da Da Da Da!
(Lynn stood up for this and holding her arms out said it *loud*!)
We thought they were shooting blanks.
It seemed like an eternity before the ambulances came.
It felt like time was just standing still.
We still thought they were firing blanks.
People were on the ground bleeding, carnage everywhere.
It seemed like eternity before the ambulances came.
It felt like time was standing still.
We were right there by Prentice Hall.

KM: Yes, time seems to move more slowly under stress...
LB: Yes, there's a distortion.
I remember where I was exactly, where the kids were. ... Let's say... I still remember that sound:
Da! Da Da Da Da Da Da Da!
(Lynn repeated the sound, with repetitions and cadence exactly as before, and I knew I was in the presence of something very real, authentic). Lynn was attempting to communicate her experience to me in every sense that John Dewey described. The subject and object of her experience were precarious, not just a series of events but temporal, changing, and historical. Her experience was also qualitative, having an immediate "brute" quality that renders it different from the usual, the mundane. Lynn did her very best to communicate that which is likely uncommunicable. In doing so, she gave me a glimpse into the past. Dewey writes that history and life have the same f*ullness:*

> The scope of "history" is notorious: it is the deeds enacted, the tragedies undergone; and it is the human comment, record and interpretation that inevitably follows. Objectively, history takes in rivers, mountains, fields and forests, laws and institutions; subjectively, it includes the purposes and plans the desires and emotions, through which these things are administered and transformed.
> (Stuhr, 2000, p. 463)

At that point, Lynn was visibly agitated, and I suggested we should stop. I turned off the recording, and we sipped our coffee. A sweet black Labrador retriever named Lola wandered about, hoping for attention, and I patted her head on each pass. Lynn talked about teaching English and language arts at the Hudson Middle School. She was very artistic in her life, creating beautiful home surroundings. Lynn enjoyed trips to Provincetown in the summer to work in an art studio there, also teaching classes in drawing, painting, and printmaking. She worked in a Cleveland studio every Wednesday. I gave her two small vintage art books printed in France, and she gave me a book of poems about Kent State. We talked about art and poetry for a half-hour, and then it was time t*o leave.*

Author's note: Sound is subjective. Aural perfection is never attainable, even by audiophiles.

Some speakers sound rehearsed, two-dimensional, but not Lynn. Her voice was a curious mix of objectivity and subjectivity. It had a kind of split personality, expressive and fluid. When she talked softly, there was a spiritual quality, like a classical guitar. When she stood up and shouted the sound of the gunfire, expression and passion emerged, like a Pete Townsend power chord.

Was there ever a recording that captured those terrible moments as well? Not to me. Lynn's voice was warm and gutsy, with harmonics and passion. It added realism, excitement, and dimension to the story, a curious mix of the objective and the subjective. It was warm, cold, or brittle, depending on her place in her story. Lynn was a natural orator. Good teachers possess this quality, the ability to use their voice as a tool. When I recall Lynn standing and speaking in her kitchen, I feel a sense of awe. It was as if I were standing on Blanket Hill, right there in 1970, watching the National Guard march past me up the hill, turn, and fire. I've never heard anything like it before or since, and Lynn was resolute. The volume, the intonation, the delivery She remembered the sights and sounds with accuracy, something that required a special sensitivity. I could *feel* it.

Lynn was sensitive, not in the traditionally understood sense. Dominick LaCapra suggested that working through

> is in general an articulatory practice with political dimensions: to the extent one works through trauma and its symptoms on both personal and sociocultural levels, one can distinguish between past and present and to recall in memory that something happened to one (or one's people) back then while realizing that one is living here and now with openings to the future.

Figure 7.2 May 3, 1970. Pictured are two guardsmen and a police officer at the intersection of Main Street and Terrace Drive. In the background is White Hall. Further back is Engleman Hall, at that time a women's dormitory (photograph courtesy of Paul Gailey).

Lynn provided a virtuoso performance, making real what had remained abstract, to "see" the past and future around the curves in the river of time, to where the hidden past came into view.

I later paired her voice with the enhanced recording Alan had unearthed in the Yale University archives. While not perfect science, the cadence and intonation seemed to match. Lynn animated – breathed life into – what happened on *that* hill, *that* day, *that* time *that* place. As an artist and teacher, her individuality was tied to the shootings. Lynn spoke to others through her teaching and her art. Her recounting of May 4 was an experience in every sense of the word. No longer abstract, it became – for a few minutes – a concretization, visible and real through her voice, countenance, and presence. When I left that afternoon, I felt as if the past had been reactivated in the present day. I contemplated a future that lay beyond and hope to find it.

References

Eisner, E. (1992). *Education artistic vision*. Macmillan: New York.
Pinar, W. F. (1978)
Stuhr, J. (Ed.) (2000). *Pragmatism and classical American philosophy: Essential readings and interpretive essays*. Oxford University Press: New York.

8 Nancy Csernotta Joyce

Karl: I'm so glad you called!

Nancy: I'm glad I caught you! I was just thinking about you and realized that I was going to call you I never did. I had a moment right now and wanted to do what I said I said I would.

Karl: Do you mind if we revisit…you were in your dorm on Monday, May 4?

Nancy: Yes, but let me backtrack. What happened was…I was there, I was there for the weekend, but we had friends that were getting married, so we drove to Cleveland on Sunday morning to go to their shower because…I think I told you we were in the bars in downtown Kent on Friday night. Everyone was drinking, celebrating. We were in The Loft, on the corner. The police closed all the bars and made everybody go back home. And so, there were hundreds of kids pouring out into the streets that night, which was a not a smart thing for them to do.

Karl: And that was Friday night?

Nancy: Friday night, yes! All these kids who were drinking were put out into the streets, and they had to leave and go home.

By the way, we were there for the weekend. And my husband and I – he was in college at that time too…and then Sunday morning we drove to Cleveland because we had friends that were getting married. We were there for their wedding shower. And my brother-in-law and sister-in-law who were living in the married student housing where Lynn and Archie lived, they drove with us to Cleveland, went to the shower, and then we drove back late Sunday night.

When we got back late Sunday night, they wouldn't let us on campus. The National Guard had all the roads blocked because of the ROTC issue, the burning of the ROTC building, which happened Saturday night, and whatever else was going on. Right? Right. So, we couldn't get back on campus. We had to

Figure 8.1 Pictured are the guardsmen, a Jeep, and an armored personnel carrier by Summit and Lincoln Streets. (photograph courtesy of Paul Gailey, May 3, 1970).

drive back to Cleveland, and then we drove back Monday morning because we all had classes.

Monday morning, we got back, and I went to my dorm, and I was up there washing my hair, getting ready to go to my class in the afternoon. And…and then I heard the gunshots. … I didn't know specifically that they were gunshots, but it sure sounded like it, you know? And then…I was in the dorm, and my husband was on the roof of Allen Hall because he was the, he was a residence advisor there.

He watched things happen. from up there. But anyway, we all heard the gunshots. I got ready for the day, and then I don't remember, I mean, we didn't have email in those days, so must have been announcements through the dorm that everything was closing down and everybody had to go home, and my parents weren't able to come to Kent until the next day to get us.

They closed all the roads coming in, so people had to identify who they were to come and get their children. And I went to Lynn and Archie's apartment and spent the night, and then my dad came and got me the next day.

Karl: Well, they were over in what, Silver Oaks then? Is that what those apartments were called at that time?
Nancy: Silver Oaks. Yeah. That's where my brother-in-law and sister were living. He heard the, the shots come. Some of those bullets hit those buildings over there. I don't know if you knew that.
Karl: I didn't know they reached that far! This is good information.

Nancy:	You know, that's what he said. I don't know if that's true, but he said some of the bullets hit…they hit some of the buildings that far away.
Karl:	You mean all the way to Tri-Towers and beyond, right?
Nancy:	Yes. The side of some of the buildings at Silver Oaks. That's how far some of them went. They were using M1 rifles, right?
Karl:	Yes. From what I've heard it is a very powerful weapon.
Nancy:	Yes, which was part of the controversy about having the National Guard there, these young guys with those powerful guns on a college campus.
Karl:	Lynn felt that National Guard shouldn't have been there.
Nancy:	Yeah. They shouldn't have been there. Well, they fired at a bunch of college kids, you know what I mean? The college kids weren't being violent, but according to everything I've read, there was a subversive group on campus traveling around the country…stirring things up in places. And then they came to the little sleepy town of Kent, and that's where the big event happened. Like most of us there, we knew there was protesting going on and the war and all that stuff, but people, people I knew and the kids around me…I mean, they weren't violent, and you know what happened that day was just kind of a freak accident.
Karl:	Well, where I'm sitting in the car right now, across from what now is FedEx, but it used to be Perkins Pancake House. Do you remember that? Apparently, a lot of their windows were broken. I don't know about Captain Brady's. On campus, most of the people – including Lynn – didn't feel that there were an awful lot of rocks that people could have picked up and thrown at the guard.
Nancy:	Yes. I mean…it was all…the campus was all grass and sidewalks through there, you know? There weren't a lot of rocks to pick up and throw.
Karl:	Well, I've been up in the archives a lot…going through boxes. I know there are a few rocks in boxes that were numbered, and even shell casings. I stumbled across these artifacts quite by accident. Even the archivists didn't know what was in those particular boxes. I didn't get to talk with Lynn in person more than twice. We talked and texted every month or so, texted on the phone. She finally decided it would be all right to talk with me, and she was very generous. I wanted to ask, Have you read that book *The Body Keeps the Score*?
Nancy:	No, I haven't.
Karl:	The author writes about PTSD and how different the impact is on individuals. Is it possible that *all* the people that were there – on site – have internalized some trauma? I'm not a psychologist, but it makes sense to me. You certainly knew Lynn better than I

	did, but she thought that there were some repercussions, something that stayed with her. And I'm sure that part of Lynn's teaching – her empathy and compassion – were formed by her experiences on May 4. What do you think?
Nancy:	You know, I think for all of us that were there, whenever May 4 came around, it was a very emotional day for years and years and years. It could be because you never forgot, you know, how awful that was that happened in a place where you were spending so much time, so much of your life.

When they did the 50th remembrance a couple years ago, I listened to it. I put it on. Maybe it was taped or something. It was a couple hours long. I listened to it while I was doing some things in the house, and I was so depressed. It was so sad. I just felt, I felt like crying because of what happened and those, those young people who never got to live and it was senseless, the whole thing was, you know, it was just senseless…

So…so it…it's a memory. I mean, you never forget. You know what I mean? And when May 4 comes around, I always think… Oh my God! It's May 4! You remember, right? It's just one of those dates that sticks out in your mind. Yeah. I remember so well that day on the 50th commemoration, commemorative service, or whatever they did that day.

I listened to the whole thing, and I remember calling Lynn, and we were both, well. … She had the same feelings. We were both so sad and depressed that day, listening to the recordings of the parents of those kids, and they interviewed a lot of people for that occasion.

Karl:	Nancy, those are poignant reflections. Very touching…
Nancy:	Yes. It was just, it was *very* touching, but it was very, very sad.
Karl:	Very emotional. You know, Lynn seems to be, or seemed to be. I'm sorry. You know, she was a lovely person, wasn't she?
Nancy:	Yes. She was…was truly a lovely person…
Nancy:	While you're thinking about that, this is kind of interesting because my grandson is 12 years old, and he goes to a private school in Cincinnati, and they actually studied…they were studying *Ohio history* and they brought up Kent State. He asked me about it. He asked me if I was there. Isn't that interesting that in school at 12 years old, it's part of Ohio history?
Karl:	Extremely interesting! Jerry M. Lewis wants me to work with him on a curriculum for teaching Kent State to upper elementary kids. He wrote a lengthy manual about how to teach May 4, but that was for high school seniors. I'm guessing that your grandson was in sixth grade when he was studying that history. I wonder how they presented it.

Nancy: I have no idea. I don't know, but he asked me about it, and I was so impressed that it was part of their Ohio history

Karl: I wonder how the school presented "both sides." I don't believe Lynn would've thought that there were two sides, but I asked Jerry about that. I believe his position was that the guard shouldn't have been there on campus. He asked that I try to picture what was in their minds when the shooting happened. Some were aiming right into the parking lot at the students, but some fired into the air or into the ground. They couldn't bring themselves to shoot kids.

Nancy: Exactly. Because guess what? How old were those guys when they were deployed on campus. Weren't they in early 20s? They were young people too.

And there were a lot of people there on campus and locally, a good number from our family. I was there. Lynn was there. Archie was at work. My brother-in-law was there, but I think he must have been in his apartment. My sister-in-law was a nurse at Robinson Memorial because she had already graduated.

Karl: Lynn told me that she and her sister would go into Cleveland on Wednesdays to do artwork and printmaking.

Nancy: Right. They went to Cleveland every Wednesday to do art making, and that sister has since moved here by me.

Karl Martin: Your family seems close and supportive.

Nancy: Luann is that sister's name. She lived in Kent for a long time. Her husband was a professor at the university. Maj Ragain. He's part of the. ... He was part of the...what was it called...*Jawbone*. Do you know about *Jawbone*?

Karl: Yes. It's a program offered by the Wick Poetry Center, correct?

Nancy: Yes, *Jawbone*. ... Maj was a poet. He was a professor at Kent. I don't know if he was there when May 4 happened. I think he might, might have been, but he has since passed away. He was a big poet, well-known at Kent State University and the Wick Poetry Center. Every spring they tied into the May 4 weekend.

Karl Martin: I know the director, David Hassler. I was his art teacher at Longcoy Elementary School.

Nancy: Yeah, David, I know him too. He is a good friend of Luann's. David and Maj were best friends

Karl Martin: Yes! He's done great work at Kent State. But, on that subject – poetry – when I went over to see Lynn at her home... she brewed a cup of coffee and then we talked for about a

	half hour. She shared her story, and I turned off the recorder. I had taken two small art books as a gift, and she wanted to give me something. She looked around the house, handed me a book, and said, "I want you to have this". It was a book of poetry, and it was signed. I'm going to try to locate it today.
Nancy:	That must be Maj's book. I'll bet it's Maj Ragain's book, and he signed them all.
Karl:	Well, it's so good that we're talking, bringing everything around full circle now.
Nancy:	Maj was one of David's best friends, and they did a big tribute to him this past spring for May 4. There was a painting that was donated in Maj's name at the Wick Poetry Center.
Karl:	So, Maj was more than a poet. He was family.
Nancy:	Yes. My youngest sister Luann…He was my youngest sister's husband. You met Luann on that walk at Kent State with Lynn. He was a professor at the university for years and years and years. I think he was there on May 4. He died four years ago. They did this big dedication to him at the Wick Poetry Center because he was very involved there.
Karl:	Well, as it turns out, Lynn gave me a precious remembrance, and I think I can connect some dots with what you've shared.

Figure 8.2 In the background is the well-known Lincoln entrance of Campus Supply. (photo courtesy of Paul Gailey).

Nancy: There you go. I don't know if Maj ever wrote about May 4. I'd have to ask Luann, but maybe there's something in that book.

Karl Martin: I'll let you know. I'll revisit it and send a picture to you.

Nancy: It's one of his books. I'm trying now to think how many signed poetry books she had from other poets. It's got to be from Maj Ragain.

Karl: The funny thing is, when I met Lynn during Alan Canfora's tour, I had this strong feeling like I knew both. They both were friendly and kind.

Nancy: I know exactly what you mean. Please let me know when the book is published.

References

Hopcke, R. H. (1992). *A guided tour of the collected works of C. Jung.* Shambhala: Boston, MA.

Jung, C. G. (1966/1978) *The spirit in man, art, and literature.* Princeton University Press.

9 John Cleary, Architect

John gladly met with me on three occasions to share his experiences and insights. His memory of the violence of May 4, 1970, is vivid and rich in detail. One might think that memories would become less precise and generalized over time. It doesn't seem as if John's memory changed with time and circumstance, and he seldom pauses to remember salient details or the chronological arrangement of events.

In its simplest form, memory is about information retention over time. It is an integral part of human cognition since it enables individuals to recall and draw upon past events to frame their understanding of and behavior in the present. Memory represents our collective and individual past to function in the present and the future: "Without it, we are condemned to an eternal present. That memory persists after an experience suggests that an internal representation of this experience is stored in the brain and that later this representation can be reconstructed and used" (Josselyn & Tonegawa, 2020, p. 2).

John Cleary is a retired architect. Shot in the chest on May 4, he was featured on the cover of *Life Magazine* on May 6, 1970, being attended to by students. His generosity and warmth were evident throughout our sessions. He believes that he was spared extra trauma because he was knocked unconscious from being center-shot. That was his own testimony. John wasn't awake to see the carnage and subsequently had surgery at Robinson Memorial Hospital.

John didn't return to participate in May 4 commemorations for 15 years. What prompted him to return was a coincidental, compelling, personal event: the birth of his son 15 years later – on May 4. John believed that was a calling, that he had to go back, reengage with the May 4 community, and deal with what happened to both the country and him. John acknowledged his injury and trauma, his memory of the people and happenings sharp until the critical moment. In writing historically, I respect his authority without question, without coarsening his valuable recollections. In a real sense, he accomplished the impossible. John survived a horrible trauma without losing touch with his identity. According to Friedlander

DOI: 10.4324/9781003399094-9

Figure 9.1 Photograph courtesy of John Cleary, from his freshman year, spring 1970, with longer hair, mustache, and goatee.

(1992), "Deep memory and common memory are ultimately irreducible to each other. Any attempt at building a coherent self founders on the intractable return of the repressed and recurring deep memory" (p. 41).

His sincerity surfaced as he described the humanity of students forming a cordon around him, holding hands to protect him from the guardsmen. At that time, they were risking their lives because no one knew what the guard would do next. A few minutes later, they were instructed to fire again to disperse a crowd of 200 students who were seated and refusing to move. More tragedy was averted due to Professor Glenn Frank's impassioned plea for the students to leave – and leave quickly.

Perhaps John's story alludes to a repressed past, perhaps not. This will be explored further, but I believe that under the stress or fear of the repetition of the negative experience, many who were present just moved on. This may have reduced the chances that there will ever be communication leading to a foundation of feeling and equality upon which an understanding can be built.

My first interview with John Cleary is a good summation of the events of May 4 as they unfolded. I encouraged him to revisit his past, to work from stories to possibilities through our relationship, through our dialogue:

Karl: Hi John, thanks so much for agreeing to an interview.
John: No problem. I'm sorry I called a little late. We were just sitting around with our third cup of coffee and lost track of time.
Karl: That's fine. It gave me a chance to review a few things. Where would you like to begin?

John: Let's back up to Friday. I'd like to start with Friday night because it sets the stage well as to the way things happened. Friday night, I was supposed to study difficult material with some friends for a class. I lived in Stopher Hall that year, as a freshman. We had heard that there were some incidents on campus and in town.

Sunday was a beautiful day. Spring had pretty much been cold and wet.

I was always a camera buff, always had an SLR on hand, but for some reason, I borrowed my roommate's "point-and-shoot" Instamatic. I always loved taking pictures, so this wasn't remarkable.

So...the guardsmen began to advance. They started firing tear gas. I guess the students were able to pick up the tear gas and throw it back at the guardsmen. So, there was kind of this pitch and catch of the tear gas.

The guardsmen continued to advance, and it was a game of catch. They would fire canisters of tear gas, and the students would throw it back at the guard.

And...like I said there were a couple hundred "die-hard" protestors on the Commons but there were probably a couple of thousand students that were just basically on the hillside...and around Blanket Hill just watching what was going on.

There were many more who were just...basically...on the hillside at the Commons and around Blanket Hill just watching everything.

At noon basically, the classes changed, so you had a lot of students who were coming across campus going to their next class and, you know, seeing what was going on. They stayed to satisfy their curiosity, and a lot of people were transient, going from one end of campus to the other.

So, you did have a large body of students who were there to see what was going on. The guardsmen continued up to the top of the hill. They effectively moved the students away from the Commons down to a parking lot near Taylor Hall.

There were two companies...I can't remember offhand which was G and which was C, but once at Taylor Hall, they kind of paused on the high ground. The other company then came past the Pagoda on the other side of Taylor Hall.

Rather than stop on the high ground, they continued to march down to a parking lot in front of Taylor Hall, surrounded on two sides by a chain-link fence. They couldn't really go any further than that. Effectively boxed in by some chain-link fences, no retreat was possible from there. They were between two fences.

They found themselves on the practice football field. Again, they were boxed in by a couple of fences, and they couldn't really go any further than that.

They kind of regrouped at that point.

I saw them kind of wheel and aim into the parking lot...

in a threatening way toward the students.

And...then they huddled, and there was a group that kind of talked amongst each other.

They reformed and began to retreat up the hill, towards the crest of the hill between Taylor Hall and the Pagoda.

And...my feelings were at the time were that things were pretty much over. A lot of the students at that time were going to their next class...

It felt like things were breaking up.

It seemed like a lot of the students were leaving. There was still a lot of chanting and yelling from the parking lot.

I was getting ready to go into Taylor Hall.

I walked over near the entrance to Taylor Hall.

And I thought that I would take a picture, *one last picture* of them...as they reached the crest of the hill before they went over the other side.

So...I was advancing the camera...getting ready to take the next picture...and as I was getting ready to bring the camera up to take the picture, they suddenly turned and fired.

It didn't seem like there was any warning or shouts like, "Get back or we'll shoot" or any kind of command to shoot that I could hear. It was just like they turned and fired on cue.

There weren't really any students at all close to them.

There was one person in front of me, Joe Lewis, and myself, and the rest of the people were closer to the parking lot than the guardsmen

I was hit in the chest.

It felt like I had been hit with a sledgehammer.

It just really knocked me down...and...

pretty much I was unconscious at that point.

I was knocked unconscious.

And the next thing I remember I was in the hospital, and things were pretty chaotic.

And...I must have been in triage, because...

I just remember being afraid because in all the confusion and chaos going on in the hospital...I was afraid that I would be *forgotten*. Eventually, I went into surgery, and the next thing I remember, I was in a hospital room.

I think what happened to me was…I saw that it was a pretty close call. One or two inches either way and I wouldn't have survived. This made me feel like I was given a second chance at life, and I really devoted myself to my studies when I got back. I tended to put it behind me…

For many years, I didn't get back to Kent…I kind of buried myself in my work.

Later when I had a family, I had a tendency not to think about it. Living in Pittsburgh was good because it was far enough away that people didn't know what had happened to me there or maybe never understood. In Ohio, most people have strong feelings about what happened on May 4, one way or the other. In Pittsburgh and the surrounding area, it was easy to kind of blend into the woodwork,

And then…and this is kind of a coincidence…my son was born on May 4.

Karl: Sounds like a sign to me! Amazing!

John: Yes. I like to say that I'm a religious person…I have a strong faith. At that time, I felt that God was telling me that "you can't put this behind you," that I had to deal with it. And not bury it like I had, so…

I began to gradually come back to the May 4 anniversaries.

That was the beginning…

At first, I was a little apprehensive because I was thinking that, you know, a lot of people had been much more active than I was. I didn't know how I'd be accepted by the community because I hadn't attended any of the commemorations15 years.

When I decided to come back, a lot of the wounded students reached out and were very warm and friendly, and the May 4 Task Force would have a breakfast on the morning of May 4, and, uh…I began to attend those where we got to talk and get to know the other wounded students.

Alan reached out to me, and he and Tom were both big baseball fans, so we went to a Pittsburgh Pirates game together.

We all had a great time and…

Jim Russell has since passed on.

He was very warm and engaging talking about his life in Washington – out there…

So…gradually I started to attend, to go back to more commemorations I would say for the past 25 years I've gone to every May 4.

What I learned was that in walking around the parking lot toward the commemoration or even after you'd run into people… obviously, at our age… people quickly pick you out as being older and know that you probably were there and had some sort of involvement.

And some people probably recognized me from the cover. There was a gap that was missing...because I passed out from being shot and didn't witness the carnage, the blood, and the bodies. I was spared that in that respect. When I talk to people on May 4, maybe I run into them in the parking lot or on campus, the one common denominator is they want to share their story...and a lot of these people are hurting...because they saw things that were hard and they want to share that memory, and so they're filling in these missing pieces, and their experiences and everything become woven into this complete story about what happened on May 4.

I met with Howard Ruffner a couple of years ago, and he lives in California now, and so he just recently wrote a book with his pictures in it, and we got a chance to meet and talk...

There were a series of photographs and that one happened to make the cover of *Life* magazine.

But there was *another* that really made an impression on me.

Author's note: We were interrupted, having to continue the interview a few hours later.

John: I do some Q and A presentations with high schools in Ohio, and I have enough experience and time in that that my memory stayed recharged. I know exactly what happened, and I can communicate it well.

Karl: Absolutely! It's good to hear your voice – your inflections – as you tell your story.

John: Part of my motivation these days is to keep history alive. As we get older and older, there are fewer people concerned with the events around. I hope to keep – to let the next generation know what happened at Kent State. It's helpful to give them a firsthand look at what happened.

There is a lot of ignorance of what happened in the '70s and '80s, and it's good to give them a perspective on what happened.

Karl: That is valuable work you're doing. To me, you're writing your journey through the method of currere.

Author's note: I am encouraging John in revisiting his past – his stories, insights, and hopes. This is part of his currere journey because it ties into the regressive step in the method of currere, as one returns to the past. It's good at that point not to interpret it.

John: Can you remind me again what the Method of Currere is?

John Cleary, Architect 77

Karl: Yes. It is a four-step process, an engaging self-examination. The steps don't always have to be undertaken in order, but they are:

1 The regressive
2 The progressive
3 The analytical
4 The synthetical

My take is this: you're involved with both the regressive and progressive. You're involved with educational experiences, both inside and outside classrooms. You've allowed yourself to begin free associating as you tell your story. I'm recording what comes from it so that you don't have to. In the progressive, for example, you might imagine a better future by sharing your perspectives on what happened.

Karl: So…where are you right now? Are you relaxed on a couch or comfortable chair? In a good place? You seem to be.

John: I've got an office, and I'm quite comfortable there. When I retired, I did a couple years of consulting for a couple of years, but then the technology got beyond me.

Drawing takes up tremendous memory. …There are new software programs. I still keep my second-floor office. I'm on the computer a lot working on things and answering emails.

It's a great place to relax and get a few things accomplished.

And so…gradually, I've started to go to more and more reunions and May 4 symposiums.

Over the past 20 or 25 years, I've attended most of them.

And I've noticed – whether walking around the parking lot – or on the site before the commemoration…that people seek you out when they see the gray hair and know you probably were there and had some sort of involvement, connection, or interest.

And some people recognize me and just talking with the people who were there

There is a gap in what I know…because I was shot and unconscious, I was spared in that respect of the trauma of seeing blood, dead, and dying people in the parking lot.

I was spared that, and I guess I was lucky too.

When I talk with people on campus, on May 4, whether in the parking lot or on other areas on campus, what I notice is that – what the common denominator is – they want to share their story…

And a lot of these people are…are *hurting* because they saw things that were hard to see.

Something is missing that they want to find…their experiences…have become woven into the complete story of May 4.

That was Howard Ruffner's photograph that was on the *Life* magazine cover. I met with Howard about four years ago. He lives in California now. He just recently wrote a book, kind of a pictorial history...

And that picture's in it. There's another, that has more meaning to me than the *Life* cover, the students forming a cordon around me, arms and hands linked, after I was shot, kind of protecting me. There was a real fear that the guards were going to come back and so that photo has a lot of meaning to me, because at the time you didn't know what the guardsmen were going to do. ... They (the students) were risking their lives to protect me.

And...I don't think anyone...

I don't think anybody said, "Hey, let's form a circle around him." There was no planning. *It just happened! Linking hands and arms around me to form a circle around me...*

While Joe Cullum and the others worked on me...

That had an impact on me...

Pictured is a circle of students surrounding John Cleary, an injured student. Joe Cullum and other students are administering first aid.

And, once again, this helped to fit another piece of the puzzle together for me to understand how things happened...

What people did and how they acted.

Figure 9.2 Ronald P. McNees. News Service May 4 photographs. (Kent State University Libraries. Special Collections and Archives).

	There is a picture that Howard Ruffner took of those people in a circle, and...to me...that picture has more meaning to me that *any* others in the *Life* magazine.
	I have a copy, and I'll email it to you when we're done.
Karl:	Whatever happened to the camera that you borrowed?
John:	During the civil trial I saw pictures that I took, and a lot of the pictures that I took were basically of the guardsmen kind of crossing by me, and...some of the students, just kind of...

I tried...a couple of years ago...to access those pictures through the Freedom of Information Act,

But after going through several months of red tape, I eventually got a response, and basically, they said they couldn't find them. So...who knows? They were used in that trial, and I don't know what happened to them afterwards. But I tried to get copies of them. They were confiscated as evidence and used in the trial, so I don't know what happened to them.

Again, I tried to get copies of them but to no avail.

John submitted a proposal for a memorial on the May 4 site, overlooking the Commons. It is fabulous, allowing for reflection and contemplation in the space. Perhaps the judges believed that he was too "close" to the site to objectively be considered for the distinction.

They were confiscated as evidence and used in the trial, so I don't know what happened to them.

Again, I tried to get copies of them but to no avail.

When I was looking for an architecture program when I was in high school, we were looking at various colleges, and my dad worked at General Electric – almost everybody worked there – and he had a co-worker whose son went to Kent in architecture. I remember going over. … He invited us over to his house, and his son had all these drawings and models of stuff they had done in class, and I was just blown away...this is great, you know? And so, I was really pumped up...

So that's how I was introduced to Kent. We went out that summer and looked at the campus, and it was just a real...

It felt like just the right fit. I liked the campus, the buildings, the open spaces, and layout of the campus. It just really appealed to me. It was a great opportunity.

As a senior in high school, everybody wants to get a new start, to go somewhere where nobody knew you, and...just start fresh, so it was very appealing to me.

Karl: It *is* a beautiful campus. Even though things have filled in, a lot of the original buildings are still there, albeit remodeled a bit. The brick colors and patterns from construction in the 1950s and 1960s have new windows and trim, but they retain that "look."

John: Yes, I really like the new Promenade. ... It is Promenade or Esplanade?
Karl: Esplanade.
John: That was a great addition to the campus! What is it called?
Karl: The Lester Lefton Esplanade.
John: Right! Named after a recent college president. The primary issue they had when I was there was that the front campus wasn't effectively tied into the newer part and the recently – completed Student Center and everything. You know, it's funny...I watched the student union being built when I was a freshman, and then I worked for an architectural firm in Pittsburgh, and we got a request – a proposal – from Kent. They wanted to remodel the food court and other areas of the student union, so I got to see it built, got to see the renovations after it was updated.

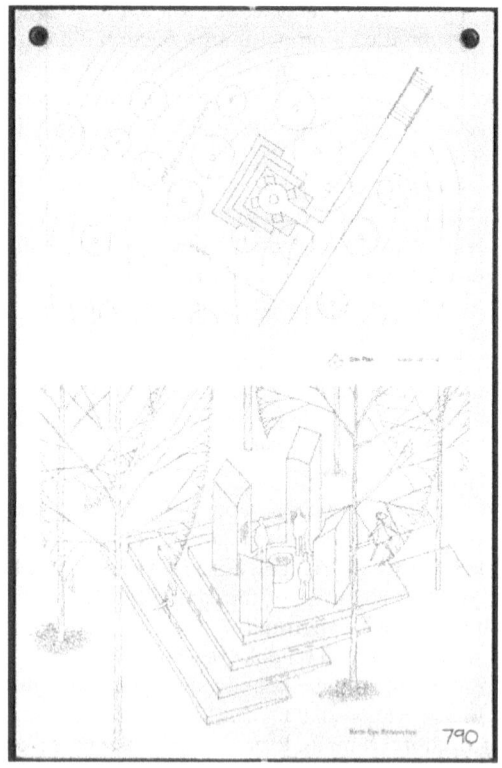

Figure 9.3 Original design of a potential May 4 memorial, by John Cleary.

John Cleary and persons interviewed shared specific autobiographical stories as the first step in the method of currere. I am encouraging them to progress, analyze, and synthesize this regressive information of their lives, to provide more than a snapshot. To move into the realm of currere, I believe it needs to explore the educational specifics of their experiences and, sometimes, revisit the trauma. They are the true protagonists in this inquiry. Regrettably, some have passed away since I began this work. I'm left with their wonderful reflections and insights, and to write elements of their the currere *for* them, on a journey they can no longer make. John Cleary is alive and well, generously sharing his experiences, photographs, and insights. I trust his memory, at least as far as *any* memory may be considered as fact.

As presented earlier, Saul Friedlander described an individual recounting of the *Shoah* as *not* pointing to redemption, *not* linear: "Each individual testimony remains a story unresolved. The overall narration is neither linear nor circular; it is a spiral recoiling upon itself, then moving into new territory through a succession of forays" (Friedlander, 1992, p. 43). This was 50 years after the fact, roughly the same period as we are concerned with here. It is hoped that this writing engenders more than archetypal responses, something here more enduring. I trust that we have ventured into new territory, a currere "exchange."

References

Friedlander, S. (1992). Trauma, transference and "working through" in writing the history of the Shoah. *History and Memory*, 4(1), 39–59.

Josselyn, S. A., & Tonegawa, S. (2020). Memory engrams: Recalling the past and imagining the future. *Science*, *367*(6473), eaaw4325.

10 Joe Cullum

Karl: Hi, Joe. Are you there?
Joe: Yep. I'm here.
Karl: You said you'd moved away from Kent?
Joe: Yeah. I was only around Kent during the four years as an undergraduate, but I was back over the years to get other degrees. I was always a commuter and have socialized in Kent a lot. As you know, for years now, it's been a place to go for live music.
Karl: I've probably seen you around. Maybe at the Loft back during the 1970s? Or even the Water Street Saloon?
Joe: I guess my most recent trip into Kent, I might have eaten in the Venice at the Erie Street Kitchen.
Karl: That ties in teaching and learning because the owner's wife, Alicia Crowe, was one of my professors about ten years ago at Kent State. Now she's a dean. I'm assuming you're in Ohioan then because you went to Kent State?
Joe: Yes. I was raised in Canton with a short foray at Ohio State and decided that the megalopolis was a bit too much for me. I dropped out at Ohio State after a quarter, and then the following spring started at one of the branches at Stark County.

And then, for my sophomore year, I went up to campus and I was there for three years. And after graduation moved away. I was in Massachusetts for five years, moved back to Ohio, and eventually decided to find something else to do with my bachelor of arts and political science.

…And started working on my education certification. Ultimately, I started teaching in my early 40s.
Karl: That is wonderful! There are few professions more valuable than teaching.
Joe: I agree. It was always something I was interested in doing. I also spent a semester at Tufts, in Massachusetts. I was in a graduate program, but things got complicated, partially personally and partially motivational.

I started thinking more about teaching high, but of course, there was a glut of teachers. So, it took quite some time before I finally got a half-time teaching job. I did that for four years, and I kept working on my master's in education at Kent. I met a guy who later became a colleague and through him got an interview for a full-time job, teaching in Minerva. That is almost on the edge of Appalachia, in a very southern part of Stark County.

Karl: Speaking of Minerva…quite a few Kent City Schools teachers used to meet at the "Top of the Inn," on Water Street. You know, a hotel at that time about eight or nine stories tall. At the Top of the Inn used to be this restaurant. There was this teacher who came on Fridays named Gary. He taught in Minerva, and I didn't even know where that was. We just called him "Gary Minerva," like the artist, Gary Indiana. That's how I still remember him. At the bottom of the hotel was Dino's Coffee. He was Greek, serving up great breakfasts. I went there Saturdays and Sundays for years.

I don't know when he went out of business, but I met some very cool people there, like the science fiction writer Harlan Ellison and musician Nils Lofgren. You never knew who might show up, because that was Kent's best hotel at the time.

Joe: I did eat there at least once, the breakfast place, that's been quite a while.

Karl: I'd walk in, and Dino would yell, "Teacher! Teacher!" It was like the *Cheers* version of breakfast. I know our time is limited, so may we start looking at May 4 and the surrounding days? At that time, I was a college freshman at Westminster, just over the Pennsylvania state line – 60 miles away.

Joe: Yeah. Yeah! I'm familiar with where it is, having, you know, gone back and forth across the state line from time to time. Not very familiar with the campus, and I don't think I know anyone who was a student there, but it was a small liberal arts school as I recall.

Karl: Well, you know one now. The enrollment was a little under 2,000 students. And the only thing I knew about Ohio then was you could get 3.2 beer in Ohio. I went to visit my friend Doug in Moreland Hills-near Cleveland – and we went to The Agora in Cleveland, and 3.2. beer was available for 18-year-olds.

And I'm just wondering, I'm fascinated with whatever experiences you like, might like to share. I'm sure you've told the story on numerous occasions, and I'd like to hear from you how things unfolded. If you're comfortable, I'd like to hear all about your experiences, and how those experiences changed you. I'm also curious about what traumatic effects it may have had on you.

Would you like to begin with the days leading up to May 4?

Joe: That would be fine, and I guess that would make sense. So, we'll begin at the beginning. At the time, I was a junior. I had been involved in some of the anti-war protests prior to that. I was a little bit limited, but I did participate.

I worked somewhere between 25 and 40 hours a week the whole time I was in school. So, I was away from campus a lot. Sometimes I worked in Kent, and at the time of the shootings, I was employed in Canton, loading ice cream trucks of all things. I would be in Kent for classes and a certain amount of socializing, and then I'd be traveling back and forth. For a while, I worked in Twinsburg.

I also worked at a gas station in Kent for a long time, so I probably would've been more involved in the anti-war movement if I'd had a little more time. But I suppose the first time publicly I did anything that, you know, felt like I was working with other people, with sort of a common cause was in October of 1969.

There was a fairly significant anti-war march in downtown Kent that was sort of in preparation for the big march that was to take place in November in (Washington) DC, which I also attended, along with a few colleagues from Kent. We loaded a car up and drove to DC. Wow! So that's kind of where it started.

I was not a member of SDS (Students for a Democratic Society) if there was such a thing. I guess at times there were actual membership rolls. But I guess I was a "fellow traveler" to use the language of the '50s (laughs). I liked it. I liked that I was sympathetic to the cause. And I remember the hearing at the Music and Speech building about the potential expulsion of SDS students who had been involved.

And off the top, I can't recall exactly what their so-called offense was, but after that fiasco when they essentially trapped protestors inside the Music and Speech building and arrested...I don't know...probably 60 students, I got involved in a group called the Concerned Citizens Community of Kent.

The idea of some kind of activism was something that I saw more and more as a necessity for people who had any understanding of what was going on in Vietnam with our foreign policy. That's what led me to political involvement. I was working Friday and Saturday, so I wasn't in Kent on those days – the Friday and Saturday before the shooting.

Saturday was the second of May. I was in Kent with my roommates watching when Nixon made his incursion speech. So, on the Friday before I left campus to go to work in Canton, there was a rally on the Commons, one of the things was that we would reconvene on Monday and consider joining the proposed national student strike.

Joe Cullum 85

My intention on that Friday was that, well, I'll be back here Monday, and we'll see what, as well as the burning of the ROTC building on Saturday.

But I was back in town for Sunday. I had attended the protest, the sit-in at the corner of Lincoln in May within an attempt to, the goal was to...get a conversation with the mayor and the president of the university about ending the curfew, the curfew that was called – as a result – of the burning of the ROTC building.

Right? Right. Because back then, you had to go to the library but there was a curfew in place so of course, the library was cleared out. National Guard were on, in, in town by that point. I do recall feeling a little betrayed by the conversation that went on between some sort of ad hoc student leaders.

Spokespersons for the police and National Guard said that if we would actually leave the street intersection itself and go back onto campus property, then we would have the opportunity to meet with someone to discuss this...this curfew. And of course, that wasn't accurate at all.

As soon as we got off the street, we were attacked with clubs. I had an acquaintance whose band was playing that night. So...the level of our naivete began to sink in a little bit that this may not have any negotiations, may not be exactly honorable and

Figure 10.1 The National Guard is shown to be in town and on campus. Pictured is a M114 command and reconnaissance vehicle. The Tudor-style building became *Captain Brady's Restaurant*. (photograph courtesy of Paul Gailey).

transparent. So, we were dispersed with tear gas, clubs, and bayonets, and I spent probably over an hour trying to make my way back to the apartment building where I lived over on East Summit Street. This was from the north side of, of Main Street and through the neighborhoods with the helicopters flying overhead.

This is Sunday. This is Sunday night, and I had to hide, hiding in bushes as National Guardsmen in Jeeps were going by. I assumed that they were just going to arrest anybody on site for breaking the curfew.

Karl: You made it back to your place?

Joe: I did make it back to the apartment and, ultimately – without knowing much more about what else was going on – I decided just to get some sleep and get up in the morning and go to class, which is what I did on Monday morning. It was my last class of the day. I had all morning classes so I could get to work later.

I had a German history class. I think it covered the years from post-World War I to what was then the present. It covered the whole rise of Nazism and might have started even before that. Kenneth Caulkins was the professor, and I really enjoyed him. You know, it's a little ironic.

We're talking about the rise of Nazism, and in those days, we used that word a little bit too freely to describe some of the people in the Republican party, the people that were behind the war, and, for that matter, Democrats also. The war fascism was also pretty good. Wouldn't be that much of an exaggeration to use that term.

Fascist or Nazi. Yes, those terms were used freely then. I thought it was a little ironic seeing what was happening on campus after having just spent by that time, more than half of a quarter studying the rise of the Third Reich. After that class, which was over at ten of noon, I headed over to the Commons for that rally that was planned for noon.

And I got there about the time that students were beginning to try to speak and also the National Guard was making the announcement that the assembly was illegal, that we were in violation of the riot act, and we had to disperse. This was the beginning of the firing of the tear gas.

Karl: You were over by the Victory Bell at that point listening, correct?

Joe: Yes, I was just partway up the hill, between the Victory Bell and Taylor Hall. At that point, when the tear gas started to be fired at us, I went up to the west of Taylor Hall and over the crest of the hill, as far as the practice field and the dormitories that were over on that area.

And then, ultimately the National Guardsmen stopped, turned and sort of faced people off. And there's a fairly famous photograph of Alan Canfora with his black flag. And National

Guardsmen had assumed a kneeling position aiming at him. But...then they began to return to where they originally had been, heading back up the hill between Taylor and Stouffer. And the assumption by a lot of people was that they ran out of tear gas because they weren't firing any tear gas anymore. It began to feel a little bit like sort of a victory in that they were retreating, and we had not been driven off campus.

And...at least in my mind, the thought was maybe we will still have the opportunity to consider this student strike. Of course, that all changed when they reached the crest of the Hill. By that time, I was very close to that line of 15 or 20 National Guardsmen. In fact, there were some people who were closer, but there was no one between me and them at the time.

They turned and started to fire. I was close.

Karl: You saw this happen?

Joe: Oh yeah, yeah. I was so close that my assumption was, well, they're not firing live ammunition; they're firing blanks. But I was close enough to be injured by the residue of a blank cartridge. So that's what it took for me to get on the ground, which, you know, in hindsight, I was an awfully lucky person.

Joe Lewis was pretty close as I recall. And John Cleary also.

Karl: Where, exactly, were you...your position?

Joe: I was about at the same distance from the National Guardsmen as John Cleary was.

But I was closer toward...the gym, Bowman Hall was to the South. I was probably 30 feet away from John. And so, when... when they stopped firing is when I looked up, looked around, and I looked over and the closest person I could see who was down was John Cleary. So, I...I went over to see what was going on with him.

And...I saw that he had a...a bullet wound in the chest and I...I tried to administer whatever inept first aid I could. And that is where and when Howard Ruffner took the photograph that got me on the cover of *Life* magazine, so I know...

That's me, the guy with the beard. It's now a lot grayer.

(There is a pause.)

Karl: I'm fascinated with your story Joe because you've had an experience that none of us can duplicate or possibly understand. ... Please continue.

Joe: Okay, I'll go through to the end of that day anyway. So, you know, there's a...there was no preparation for this. You would think that if there was planning by the law enforcement authorities, there might have been more preparation, but there was no preparation as far as what would happen if people were injured.

So, it took a while for any ambulances to arrive. And I stayed with John until – finally – an ambulance arrived, but there weren't enough of them. So, John was loaded on what I would call a gurney, something that was intended to be used in the back of one of those sixties' era ambulances. And yes...beside it was a seat, a long bench seat, and someone had procured a stretcher somewhere, and put another student on that stretcher, and that was placed on the bench seat.

So, myself and, and another student who I didn't know and haven't seen since, rode in the ambulance with John and this other student to keep the...keep him on the, on the seat because you know, there was no...he was not secured to that seat. The, the gurney was secured to the floor. We went over to Ravenna, and as we were getting out of the ambulance, I took the wallet out of the pocket of the student who was on the bench seat, who was laying on his side, who had been shot in the side so I could give it to the emergency room personnel to identify him.

And that's when I realized that I had gone to high school with him. It was Joe Lewis.

He was two years behind me in high school. I communicate with both Joe and John fairly regularly, even to this day. That was...that was quite an event, and I think, you know, for the first hour or so afterwards, there were things for me to do.

So, I just did those things. Whether they were much help or not, I have no idea. I think I get credited with doing more than I did. He might have...John might have been fine without what I did, probably would've been, I just tried to do *something*, and at least it kept me occupied. I was sort of focused on that, and I can't even remember how I got back to Kent.

I can't remember if I hitchhiked or if somebody else at the hospital offered a ride, but someone dropped me off on Main Street in front of...front campus. And, you know, by that time I was walking back towards where I later learned that Glenn Frank had played that significant role in disarming the situation.

But I...I wasn't there for that. I was still somewhere on the way back. And then...the rest of the day was sort of chaotic, trying to find my girlfriend, trying to find my roommates. And of course, we're all going to be driven out of town unless we had a legitimate Kent address on our driver's license.

So, I ended up taking a couple friends with me and eventually getting into Canton and staying at my parents' house until they could get back to where they lived. One lived in Pittsburgh, one over near Youngstown.

Karl: I'm sure your folks were glad to see you. How did they react to all that?

Joe: Well, my father was a World War II veteran, but he was not a Republican. He referred to James Rhodes as "Dirty Jimmy," and Nixon as "Tricky Dick." He was a union guy and a Democrat, a *New Deal Democrat*. Despite his three and a half years in military service, and my brother, who was just out of Vietnam himself – he was in the marine corps – they were both very supportive. In fact, subsequently, after the grand jury hearings and the indictments were issued, I found out that I had been indicted. I think that happened primarily because I was photographed so prominently on that *Life* magazine cover. I think they just had to identify people and pick persons to charge.

I did testify. I did testify before the grand jury; my parents bailed me out. I spent a night in jail on the second-degree riot charge, and they came and bailed me out. We were very supportive of each other. Not everybody in the neighborhood back in Canton was very supportive. I remember that the next day was the primary election, May 5, and for the first time in my life I voted because I was not yet 21, but I would be 21 in time for the general election.

So, I was able to vote, and I registered as a Republican so I could vote against Rhodes for the Senate and was happy that he didn't make it to the Senate. But he was reelected after he did a couple terms as governor, sat out one and came back.

Karl: When I talk with members of the community, I often get negative comments about the students. What was your experience?

Joe: I found it interesting that the reactions that a lot of people got – and I got – from a lot of the townsfolks. But, because I worked in Kent and I worked at this gas station, regular customers came in. The guy that owned the gas station was a World War I veteran. During World War II, he worked at the Ravenna arsenal, and in his retirement, in his 70s bought a gas station. I thought at the time he was really old. It just seemed that way. Just from spending time there with him and some of the other guys who worked there who were not students...there were a couple of us who were, and there were several who weren't. They didn't have that same attitude because they actually knew us. They actually knew people who were involved in the protest. We talked about these things, but people who didn't know students in a personal level were so quick to just make it all into something. And Governor Rhodes made comments about us being the worst we harbor in America, the night riders and, and said we were worse than the Nazi Brown Shirts.

(Author's note: The Brown Shirts were Nazi Party militia – created in 1922 – that helped Hitler rise to power. Governor Rhodes did, in fact, make these statements).

Yes...The Brown Shirts. I think people were influenced by that. But I understood some of the issues, and it had to be a little tough when Kent was growing, but the university was growing the way it did much faster, even into the '70s. The townspeople felt a little bit...that they were displaced in their town. We can see the evidence of how easy it is for people to be gullible, especially when we look at how they voted in the last election...so easily vote against their own interests if there's somebody stirring up opposition with a big megaphone. And we didn't have Fox News in those days, we had politicians who were their own propaganda arms. Well, yeah.

Karl: And you haven't even gotten to Spiro T. Agnew.
Joe: Well...he was hit man for Nixon in that campaign of 68. I think he was forced to resign, wasn't he? I guess it was the sins of the past when he was in office in Baltimore, whether he was governor earlier where he was taking kickbacks.

People think of the Republican party as the patriotic side of things, but they seem to be so often caught with their hands and the cookie jar. For example, the whole thing in Ohio with First Energy and Householder, time and time again, these holier than thou Bible-thumping, good Christian politicians turn out to be corrupt thieves.

(Author's note: Ohio House Speaker Larry Householder was charged with bribery and a conspiracy related to House Bill 6, the state nuclear and coal "bailout" law.)

Karl: Let's move back just for a minute. Is that all right? Regarding the *Life* magazine cover, there was another photograph where the students form a circle around John Cleary. You must be in that one.
Joe: I was with John from the time he was shot until we loaded him in the ambulance. There were other students that were basically protecting us I see from being trampled by any kind of crowd. I think students did that around several of the wounded people. I might be in the photograph somewhere, but I would probably be kneeling right at the base of that sculpture with John.

By the way, I knew Jeff Miller. He lived in a building behind mine. We lived in this row of student slum apartments on Summit Street. I lived in a big white house that probably had 20 students living there. It had a swimming pool and then there was a yellow house behind it. And that's where Jeff lived. We played on a softball team together.

There was a dorm league, a fraternity league, and an off-campus or commuter student softball league. We were the ones with the long hair. Because of that, I knew Jeff pretty well. But when I…I turned in Joe's identification at the desk at Robinson, I saw them bring Jeff in and I could see that he was dead. That was the first time I realized that anybody died there, and it was someone I knew.

The memories are vivid for me, and I have never avoided what I consider responsibility to tell the story. In fact, the most recent time I've talked about this was at a Kiwanis Club presentation, right here in Alliance. I volunteered at a food pantry since I've retired, and through my work there I've gotten to know a whole lot more people in Alliance than I ever would've known prior to this.

I lived five miles out of town. I never worked in Alliance, and I didn't grow up there. It was just a place where I went shopping for food. I used to go to hear some music back in the day when they had live music in Alliance. I've met a lot of people, and so I've had opportunities to talk to different groups. They tend to be baby boomers for the most part, or maybe a little younger, but a lot of them are the people who still seem to be involved in community and charitable organizations.

I've always been well received by these groups and sometimes the people in the groups have been retired police officers, FBI agents, and military.

One of the guys that I spoke with at the last Q&As – I've known him for a couple of years from volunteering at the food pantry. He's an amputee who lost his leg in Vietnam. He seems to be open, very much to be willing to listen and learn. I think it's all a part of the personal connection. If they get to know me, they can't make me an "other," because I've connected on different levels over certain things. They're more open to listening to the story.

Another thing: It's been a lesson plan for me every May 4 for all 19 years that I was teaching in high school. It fits in very nicely with 20th-century history, which I've taught, and also works with government because it's a case study about the first amendment. A lot of students that have passed through my classroom have heard this story, and I'm sure they're fascinated. I spoke to a group of history students, college students over at Akron University once, and the only negative I got with that group was from a guy who was hearing or reading about the reception of the GIs coming back from Vietnam…and how they were spat upon and called baby killers and that is something I never witnessed...ever. I also have bred from other people that it might have been apocrypha, just a way to build more animosity towards the anti-war movement. But one of the things I told him, which I think made him think a little differently is that...what really impressed me and really got me to turn the corner on my questioning about whether this war was justified in any way was hearing the stories of the guys that came back.

I have cousins and brothers and friends who were in Vietnam and even joined the Vietnam Veterans against the War. That was a very effective organization in giving credibility to the anti-war movement. They had experienced it, and I think just that connection with, uh, the group at Akron U settled that guy's mind.

Greg Miller was a history teacher who was working on oral history of May 4. I don't know if you've, you're familiar with it.

Karl: Yes, somewhat.

Joe: I did a little recounting of this story for his book and spoke in one of his classes. I think with the right perspective, people can see, that there was a lot of credibility in the perspective of the people against the war. You just dig a little deeper, look a little deeper at the history of US foreign policy.

Karl: Joe, it was difficult for you to experience what you've shared.

Joe: I think I mentioned that initially I wasn't really registering the enormity of what happened, but later, of course, I was. So there have been times when this whole series of events sort of comes back to haunt me. Hearing the narrative on the public radio station in Kent on May 4 always does something to me. I've found myself hearing that and being close to tears as all those memories come back.

Karl: Do you feel that there were any positive outcomes?

Joe: I think something positive came out of it. I, I think that was part of what drove me to get into education ultimately, although it was sort of a wayward path to get there.

Karl: It seems to me that you've contextualized your personal memories with the stories of others. Has that been helpful for you?

Joe: Well, I was a witness, but I really wasn't a victim. Only in the loss of friends and the, the injury to friends who either were physically or much more maybe emotionally scarred by all those events. I've heard this term; it's bandied around a lot – maybe a little bit too much – but people talk about survivor's guilt. I have a little of that, especially when I consider myself standing there for the first five or so seconds as they're firing a lot of ammunition. And, you know, by this time, maybe 150 feet behind me, Jeff Miller is dead. Another friend of mine was probably 300 yards

	away, Scott Mackenzie…and he was hit. He was nowhere near this. John was walking to class, you know, so there is that sense that they were probably should have been aiming at people like me if they were aiming at the protestors. But they hit people who just happened to be there.
Karl:	Jerry Lewis said that the M1 is a very powerful weapon and that they were taught how to fire it well. He said that the rounds ended up all the way over by Silver Oaks apartments, past Tri Towers.
Joe:	Well, I know that one ended up in one of the upper stories in one of the Tri Tower dorms, and then there's that film – I don't know how famous it is, but someone was filming with a super eight camera, maybe even just a standard eight-millimeter.
Karl:	Jerry gave some of the guard a pass. He said that some of the guard fired up into the air, some into the ground.
Joe:	Yeah. But some had taken a bead on individuals, you know? Joe was shot twice, once when he was already on the ground. Probably by a guy he flipped off.

So, I don't believe we shouldn't give the guardsmen much credit at all. |
Karl:	You're a thoughtful guy, Joe. I know we're getting close to one hour. How are you holding up?
Joe:	I'm fine. I can go a few more minutes. Thanks.
Karl:	There are a lot of conspiracy theories out there, some from William Gordon. From what I read; he isn't liked by the community overall.
Joe:	I read his book. I have a half dozen books on Kent State. The worst one I think is Michener's, but Gordon's is in second place.
Karl:	What didn't you like about Michener's *Kent State*?
Joe:	The fact that he just came into town – doesn't spend much time there – sees a black squirrel, and leaves. He got into the sort of conspiracies about the student underground that's plotting and planning in this house, this haunted house. I don't think that those of us who were there were part of any conspiracy. I mean, we were wide open about the fact we were opposed to the war, and he just seemed to try to oversimplify it.

And I don't think it was well researched. I found myself quoted in the book, and I never spoke to the man. It just seemed that he should have stuck to the novels. His book was sort of like a novel, filling in the gaps of what didn't happen with what you'd like to happen…trying to tie everything together. |
| *Karl:* | Interesting thought! Going back to trauma, Dr. Bessel van der Kolk wrote *The Body Keeps the Score*, and he believes that what we experience as trauma…that is may be reactivated at the slightest hint of danger. You sometimes don't even know it's there – until it surfaces. |

Joe: Yes. As I said, I witnessed it, one step removed from the real impact of people whose lives were dramatically changed.
Karl: When you give talks, I'm sure you have rapt attention. You've got mine. if we can just go back to the, the seconds before it all happened…were there watching the, the guard retreat up the hill. Do you remember them looking back?
Joe: I remember that, but it seemed that they, their, their intention was to basically end their attempt to disperse the students. From my perspective, I didn't have any what their intentions were for real. By their body language, they, they mostly had their backs turned.

They'd look back once in a while, especially if a stone was thrown and bounced up. I saw a guy that got hit in the back of the leg with a "two hopper." But for the most part, they seemed to be intent on getting back to the top of the hill, and I assume going down the other side and back to where they were, around the burned-out remains of the ROTC building.

So that the way they turned and opened fire. Now I never heard an order and I can't say that I ever saw a hand signal, but the way they turned stood out – all 15 or 18 or however many it was – as if there was an order. It was simultaneous. On cue, right on cue. I've always hoped that someday they would get to the bottom of that.

Was that something that they planned in that so-called huddle? Is that something that, you know, came down from Governor Rhodes? Or maybe came down from Nixon that, you know, find some justification and teach 'em a goddamn lesson? Right? You know, that was the thing that really grabbed me was the way that this didn't seem to be haphazard. I believe it was planned, but where, and at what level was it planned? This has always been the question. It's still in my mind, but I am pretty sure that this was not simultaneous or spontaneous. I saw them turn simultaneously. That tells me that there was something planned about it, you know?
Karl: I wonder if there's some detail in your memory that exists on an unconscious level.

How do you know that you can trust your memory?
Joe: I sure can't depend on my recent memories, I have some short-term memory loss, but I think my memory is better for things that happened in the past.

But a lot of this, you know, the constant retelling of this story over the years, which I've been doing since 1970, right? A psychologist might say that I have been reinforcing things that I thought happened the way they did, but I don't think so. Maybe there's a way to go back and reexperience that would help me remember something different or see something that I haven't recalled for the last 52 years. It's a possibility. My concern is if I'm

	reliving it, am I reliving the narrative that I've always told as opposed to the actual experience?
Karl:	That is an interesting question. Alan said that he continually *sharpened* his memory by revisiting the story, telling and retelling the story, My college girlfriend and I took a film class in a January semester at Westminster, and one of the movies was *Rashomon*. I think it was produced in 1950, a psychological thriller about memory. I remember that a samurai is murdered, and there are lots of eyewitnesses – even the spirit of the Samurai himself – and nobody can agree about what happened. I think I saw it again in the seventies, over at like the Cedar Lee Theater.
Joe:	Yeah, I think I saw it in Boston, one of those theaters like that.
Karl:	Well, the *Rashomon Effect* evolved – was generated – from Kurosawa's *Rashomon*, where contested interpretations happen because of human subjectivity in memory. I think anthropologists use it occasionally.
Joe:	Well, I've heard that eyewitness testimony is sometimes inaccurate, projecting what you wanted to see rather than what you did see. I know that a lot of criminal cases have turned out that someone was exonerated eventually or should have been exonerated.

Figure 10.2 National Guard on Lincoln Street. McGilvrey Hall is in the background. (photograph courtesy of Paul Gailey, May 3, 1970).

	Based on faulty eyewitness testimony, you know, coached by someone who's just trying to get the case closed. They don't really care who's innocent or who's guilty, they just want to have it off their desk. Right. But I guess that's a different story. But this is, you know...different.
Karl:	Right. I would certainly trust your narrative more than something that I've read. Joe, we've been at this a long time. Is it okay with you if we take a break and maybe talk again in the future?
Joe:	Sure. That'd be great. I do get into Kent somewhat regularly, so let's do that. I don't have a lot of responsibilities in my retirement, but my wife and I are looking to move to Kent. We have a small farm, and it's getting to be too much at 73 to keep up with it.

11 Roseann "Chic" Canfora

In conversation, Roseann "Chic" Canfora speaks very much as she writes – pointed and knowledgeable. In the wake of the social changes of the 1960s and 1970s, subjects like May 4 *seem* to have lost their immediacy and relevance. Chic reactivates and illuminates those dormant events and issues. Her family – like many undergraduates at Kent State – were working-class, "blue-collar" Democrats, from Barberton, Ohio. In those days, and even into the 1980s, tuition was more affordable for Ohio residents. Public universities provided a way for the children of Ohio's middle-class families to get higher education.

I inquired as to her thoughts regarding the reactionary responses of the townspeople following May 4. Chic addressed that element of the past while critiquing and dismissing what she called "newly espoused myths."

Chic: It's disheartening to hear community folks still perpetrating myths about who we were and what we did. Much of it is conjecture, hearsay or implicit bias in efforts to describe events they neither witnessed nor experienced. Because I am a teacher, at heart, I never tire of dispelling those myths, but I do lose patience with those who fabricate stories because they have no story and, for some reason, want to espouse a connection to that moment in history. I recently served on a panel discussion and was dumbfounded by the "personal" accounts of one member of the panel and another member of the audience who shared accounts that were noticeably sketchy if not blatantly false. Not only had I never heard or read about the things they recounted, but there was no way to verify their accounts – one woman purported to be one of Allison's best friends and took great liberty, not with memorializing or teaching about this extraordinary young woman who was shot dead at 19, but about recounting their own grief and making it about *their* loss, which came across as both dubious and ingenuine because nothing was said of value about Allison or the event that led to her death.

DOI: 10.4324/9781003399094-11

Figure 11.1 Pictured is the Prentice Gate with a personnel carrier and guardsmen at the main entrance to Kent State. (photograph courtesy of Paul Gailey, May 3, 1970).

That person changed their location during the shooting at least three times during the panel discussion. I felt a tinge of embarrassment that they were not the only ones on the panel who focused their remarks on themselves and what they were doing that day, without historical context, and in no way about the brave people who faced off against state-sanctioned violence in ways that young people continue to do today. One member of the audience recalled a "conversation" with the "actual" person who burned down the ROTC building – "a high school student from Ohio" – insisting that they were privy to this "truth" that no one else ev*er knew.*

But I digress. Yes, it's unsettling to hear myths about May 4 without any way of verifying even the presence of these storytellers, and I hope you are being selective in how you share and verify their stories (Roseann Canfora, personal communication, December 14, 2022).

Chic has earned the right to resent misinterpretations of the events surrounding May 4. A photograph in the archives from 1977 shows Chic in handcuffs after her arrest while protesting the building of the new gym. She has endured many sacrifices as a result of her activism. Stated another way, Chic *owns* the narrative. Chic labeled the committee panel as "storytellers," convinced that some on the panel had invented some of their testimony. This might be true, but storytelling isn't by nature duplicitous or deceitful. It is communication and a form of therapy, an oral performance that heals through narrative.

The embassy in *The Iliad* provides an example as they walk the shore to Achilles's tent. "We watch them as they find him 'delighting his heart with his shrill lyre, fair and richly wrought, with a silver bridge on it' to which he sings the glorious deeds of men while Patroclus sits opposite him in silence" (Silk, 1987, p. 39). In musical terms – beginning with consonance – Achilles moves into "dissonance" and then back again, returning to his original state. This is a circular depiction connecting beginning and end. We might consider the original state to be "nonreflective," with narrative and the lyre a means to return to the nonreflective and consonance. It is a transactional relationship. Consonance represents notes in harmony, but also an agreement between actions and opinions. Dissonance is the opposite, perhaps equally as important when advocating for justice, accuracy, and even "truth." The narrative work Chic has accomplished – informing and clarifying what happened on May 4 – has provided a form of healing. Now a lecturer at Kent State University, Chic teaches in the School of Media and Journalism, serving the Office of the President as chair of the May 4 Presidential Advisory Committee. Chic's voice has not become muted, acquiescing into a comfortable absence of comment or concern. Her beliefs and convictions are in alignment.

I interviewed Chic in her office at Kent State, with bookends of a previous class and an appointment on either end. It was somewhat formal, not stiff but exploratory. Chic spoke slowly and deliberately at first, but she was just getting warmed up. After ten minutes, Chic didn't need to pause to select the right word. She was *engaged*...

Karl: Thanks for talking with me today. This is a wonderful office, and the view is verdant, relaxing. Thank you for seeing me, talking with me...

Chic: I would normally not do an interview at the end of a day. But I thought...at least we could start the conversation, and we could meet. And then pick a day that might work for both of us.

Karl: Yes. I was thinking we might even meet up on-site on some beautiful day if...if you were comfortable with that. I do remember that Alan had invited me to join one of the tours. When I showed up that one day, he said, "I'm really glad you're coming along because it's more authentic when you're on the hill." It was drizzly that afternoon, turning to raining and stopping. He had to watch out for people. There were people in the tour that had difficulties getting around, and Alan didn't want anybody to slide down the hill. Therefore, we didn't go up the hill towards the Pagoda [00:01:00]. We walked around the building. That's where I met Lynn Beaton and her sister. I haven't talked with her sister for a time, but she said she might be

	able to share a few extra things. And one of her brothers has some photographs that he took. I know that we talked about photographs and permissions. I was surprised that you suggested that some photos are an open resource for publications.
Chic:	A lot of things are available through the Kent State archives, but John Filo has been extremely generous with his photos over the years because he really is a strong proponent of the truth. And he has taken prize-winning photos. He's never charged any royalties.
Karl:	I should check with him.
Karl:	I recently learned something about you, that you play harp. When I went on the website, I saw that you had gigs every weekend.
Chic:	Yes. I'd been playing for over 40 years and never took it up until I was 22. I didn't even own a harp but moved to New York to learn it. And I've played ever since. I almost quit because I had a teacher that put me in recitals with 6-year-olds, and I remember playing "Twinkle Twinkle Little Star" on a big stage with all these little girls and thinking I was so old, and I should have done this when I was younger and almost quit until I met a young woman who was 16 at a harp recital.

And she was really good. And I went up to her, and I said, how long have you played? And she said, four years. And I thought when I'm 26, I'll wonder how good I might have been if I give it up now. I'm 72 and I've played ever since. |
Karl:	I remember that Alan said he was a guitar player. I wonder if one of his children might take up guitar, since …
Chic:	No, not with him gone.
Karl:	I do have a formal question and response for you. I recently corresponded with a John Dewey scholar because I was interested in how people's (long) experience after a particular and important event might have changed their lives or the way they now see the event. He responded with the following insights, and I respectfully ask that you address them.

Dewey wrote that the self does not have a history but, instead, is a history. So, this is a view of the self not as some forever self-same thing, but as a process of change. He also argues that when habits do change, it is rarely a direct or immediate change but, rather, an indirect one in which the environment of an earlier habit has changed such that the old habit just does not work anymore. So, this would counsel looking for roots of change not so much "in" a solitary self but in an environment that brought about changes in habit –how a changing world produced a different habit – including habits of perception and conception.

   (Personal communication, John J. Stuhr, September 21, 2022)

Chic, given your extraordinary experience being a May 4 survivor, would you please respond to this? How have your experiences surrounding May 4 changed your life and the way you now see the event?

Chic: I think if we see…if we see life as its own history…When I look back on the 52 years since I survived at Kent State shooting, I see how much, I, as a survivor of the shootings have not only changed but how I have grown in my understanding of the event and the way that I see all of the individuals associated with the event. If you were to look back on all of the speeches, the many speeches I gave over the years on May 4, one might think I was the angriest person for the longest period of time.

I never found it easy to understand why Dean Kahler could – so early on – forgive the guardsmen or state that he didn't resent the guardsmen and I would just say, how could you not? You…you're paralyzed for life and I…I could not forgive them. That is not to say that I do to this day. Each one of those individuals made a conscious choice when he looked through the scope of an M1 rifle and made a conscious choice to not only pull the trigger but to continue doing so for *13 seconds* into a crowd of unarmed students. So…while I don't forgive them…I, for the first time in my life…would welcome any one of them to, yes, meet me on the hill and tell me what brought them to that point. I would! I spent decades not even wanting to look at them because they disgusted me so much, but I've come to realize there was something that happened in their experience, in their orders, in the expectations of them as soldiers that…that made them do that, the *unthinkable*.

I would never excuse away their doing something so diabolical, even if it was from an order to do so. I have some appreciation for the value of knowing the truth from their perspective. I remember once I, I had advocated for us to invite Robert McNamara on May 4. And a lot of my friends were like, you know, he was an architect of the Vietnam War.

It's too little too late. He, you know…he finally came to admit in his book that as architect of the Vietnam War, he knew it was, it was wrong. He knew that our, our generation was dying for nothing, but my attitude over the years became I'll take truth no matter what. Nixon took the truth to his grave, and so did Governor Rhodes. But…I stand very hopeful that there will be a guardsman who faced off with us that day who sees some value in the truth and will tell that truth before he dies. The other side of that is I also was resentful of and stood in opposition to the Kent State University administration for more than three decades. And now I work for them. I'm a professional – in – residence here because the last two administrations, starting with President Beverly Warren, owned May 4. They respected those of us who kept that truth alive and valued our contributions. They didn't resent us the way the presidents of the university before them did.

And so, I've – in my adult life – I've come to truly value the growth of others who have their own history of May 4. For that reason, I think that we're doing far more working together on May 4 than we ever did, opposing each other around the issues associated with it.

Karl: And there's still a lot of work to be done...

Chic: There is a *lot* of work yet to be done.

Karl: When I first moved to Kent, which was 1974, I started teaching visual art in Kent City Schools. I thought...this must be a liberal place, but it wasn't. Many of the experienced teachers and townspeople disliked the students and higher education in general. These are educators, teachers, siding with the forces of law and order that killed and maimed unarmed students. And...I think it was James Dickey who described a societal and political change: "The change was not gradual. You could have stopped the car and got out at the point where suburbia ended and the redneck South began." It seemed to me then that the same was true of the polarization of attitudes between town and campus. Perhaps things haven't changed much in 52 years...

Chic: There are people in the city of Kent that still believe, and they were the same rumors that were started in Chicago in 1968 during the Democratic National Convention. The identical rumors that, that the hippies were coming in, and they were going to poison the water supply.

I mean, those kinds of myths. During our anti-war movement and, and our actions in Kent, there are people today that said that we were going to put LSD in the water supply. But you know, when you have the university itself, the, the president in 1970 President White, who allowed the FBI to take over campus, that permitted, armed gunmen to come on campus.

And then he left town, left us vulnerable to attack. He was the same one who opened up our dorm rooms for them to put on display in Memorial Gym. They used anything confiscated from our rooms that would make us look like drug-crazed, weapons-carrying students. I mean, my *hiking stick was on that table*.

My roommate's prescription meds were on that table...*anything* that would brand, and exactly what [00:16:00] people wanted to believe. Middle America, who couldn't fathom that American soldiers would turn their guns on American people unless you had a good reason to do so. So...they looked for those reasons.

And that's why Brage Golding…No, it was actually Glenn Olds, who said "Five years is long enough to remember Kent State," and he ended the commemorations and that's when, as a group. My brother and a couple of the other wounded students started the May 4 Task Force that kept the commemorations going for the next 40 years.

Karl: When friends would come into town, they always wanted to see the Commons and Blanket Hill. In fact, they wanted to see everything. As you know, there were no tours then.

Chic: They didn't want us, but we've given tours for the last 52 years. There were no official ones. There were no Kent State University–sponsored tours…

Karl: No signage either. There was nothing, except the hole in Don Drumm's *Solar Totem*. And the administration wanted us to forget about the term "Kent State."

Chic: Yes, they wanted to change the name from "Kent State" to "Kent." Oh yeah. Well, ten years in rage, Brage Golding it's four. Yeah. Brage Golding (Kent State University president from 1977 to 1982) said, "Ten years is long enough to wear a hair shirt." He lied to us and in saying we were "wearing a hair shirt," he suggested that we were just an irritant.

Karl: He said *that*?

Chic: Yes, and we kept coming back. We were just an irritant that kept coming back.

Figure 11.2 Pictured are two guardsmen in a Jeep in traffic on Main Street, Route 59. The restaurant in the background has had many incarnations over the decades. (photograph courtesy of Paul Gailey).

Author's note: "Hairshirts are garments made from rough animal hair (usually that of goats) worn as a top or under a shirt so the coarse hair will rub and scratch the wearer. This discomfort serves both as an act of penitence and a constant reminder of faith so as to better avoid the temptation of sin" (Christina Garton, 9/27/2019). It seemed to me that Brage Golding's remark was condescending, unbecoming of a university president.

Finally, a philosophical account of pragmatic experience may not shed much light on the particulars. In Dewey's 1938 essay, he suggests that human nature does and doesn't change.

References

Garton, C. (2019).
Silk, M. S. (1987). *Homer: The Iliad.* University Press: Cambridge.

12 The 1970s and My Journey of Understanding

A good argument could be made that the 1960s officially ended on May 4, 1970. Professor Emeritus Jerry M. Lewis agrees, preferring to call the 1960s the "Vietnam Era" (Hensley & Lewis, 2010, p. 128). The killing and wounding of Kent State students by the Ohio National Guard definitively slammed shut the door of that decade. This ignited massive protests nationwide, and the Vietnam War officially ended following my first year of teaching, in 1975. Those were good days for a new teacher. I was younger and less experienced than my colleagues and community, but I was motivated, representing myself well as a teacher. I realized early that teachers impact thousands of lives during their careers, and I had a passion to help kids learn.

Teachers in Kent were highly regarded during the 1970s, and the community saw us as trusted professionals. Behavior modification was in vogue, objectives and outcomes spelled out in advance and tied to assessments. The teacher was reduced to a technician, artistry nonexistent and outcomes specified. I was hired, however, by someone who encouraged experimentation and a creative approach to teaching and learning. I displayed a photograph of John Dewey, and happily considered teaching visual art as a calling. Students gravitated toward me, and I was given student teachers beginning with my second year. I spent summers in Narragansett, Rhode Island, painting, surfing, and enjoying the beach.

During that time, Kent State was always there, providing excellent speakers, concerts, and opportunities for growth. It was an integral part of life and landscape. The beautiful campus, school of art, and first-rate university library were a perfect milieu for an artist and educator. I took advantage of what was offered, from lectures by Leonard Nimoy to intensive Blossom-Kent painting residencies. These offerings were taught by visiting artists and engaging professors like Harold Kitner and William Shock, who shared firsthand accounts and strong opinions about a variety of issues, including May 4. As a graduate student from the mid-1970s to the early 1980s, I recall that the history of May 4 was always part of the

DOI: 10.4324/9781003399094-12

"hidden curriculum," taught unofficially but considered seminal to our sensibilities as art students. The site and the history were just a few steps away.

Visiting family and friends wanted to see the Commons, Taylor Hall, Blanket Hill, and the Don Drumm sculpture, entitled *Solar Totem*. Those who were artists and photographers wanted to visit environmental artist Robert Smithson's *Partially Buried Woodshed* and the School of Art. Nearly all wanted to see the "Psycho House," where – according to James Michener – members of the Students for a Democratic Society (SDS) lived. This was also included in these unofficial tours, accessed by a steep driveway at night. Three of my public school students and their parents lived there for a decade, enjoying both the history and the view. "From the rooftop vantage point, large sections of town and campus were visible. It was amazing to sit out there at night!" (Jacob Vanags, personal communication, July 6, 2021).

It is unsubstantiated, but according to public memory and legend, Alfred Hitchcock saw the house at 233 Columbus Street and thought it looked "evil." Following that narrative, it became an inspiration for the Alan Bates house in the movie *Psycho*. According to the Kent Historical Society, it is known as the *Elgin House*.

Many false stories about the Elgin House sprang up after the May 4 shootings, Kent Historical Society Executive Director Guy Pemetti said. Kent was inundated with national journalists, including famous author James Michener, who wrote a book about Kent. "Michener's book falsely stated that Robert Bloch, who wrote the novel *Psycho*, lived in the Elgin House" (Garrett, 2005, p. 8).

During the 1970s and most of the 1980s, there were no commemorative markers or signage. Cars routinely parked on the areas where students fell at the lot adjacent to Prentice Hall. Except for personally invested activists like Alan and Chic Canfora, history was all but forgotten. Their mission – their lifelong vocational calling – was embodied through the curriculum: "In short, though curriculum history can promise no solutions, a rediscovery of the past can serve as a partial corrective to a long-standing characteristic of the field – that of ahistoricism" (Ponder, 1974, p. 463). The Canforas made every effort to keep the history from being forgotten, but a new issue arose. In 1976, the university proposed that a new gym be built:

> A meeting of the Kent State University Board of Trustees marked the first time all the trustees were involved in the development of the new facility. About 40 students attended. Scott Marburger, Student Caucus executive secretary, and Nancy Grimm, a Caucus representative, presented the first formal expression of concern about the site, a list of six student concerns: lack of adequate student input on all levels of the

Figure 12.1 Karl Martin at the *Victory Bell*, Winter 1978. (photograph courtesy of William Cogliano).

decision-making process; insufficient justification of the proposed facility; destruction of the natural beauty of the area; possible alteration of the May 4th site, raising legal and historical questions; need for complete and exhaustive consideration of alternative sites; and the intended source of operating and maintenance costs of the proposed facility.

(Kent State University Library. *Kent State Tent City: Gym Annex Protest Chronology*)

The Board of Trustees voted unanimously to finalize plans and to build the gym. Soon to resign, President Glenn Olds rejected the demands of the Student Coalition and May 4 Task Force. Beginning on May 12, 1977, about 60 students pitched tents on the site to protest the decision. A court order to vacate the site followed. Brage Golding arrived on campus on July 12 to assume the presidency. On August 20, a rally on the Commons featured folk singer Joan Baez and speeches by several of the parents of the dead and wounded students. About 1,500 people attended. Afterward, 600 persons marched to the Kent City Police Station to protest the previous evening's arrests of Coalition members despite a temporary restraining order.

Joan Baez

August 20, 1977, was a perfect day in northeast Ohio. Joan Baez flew in to support the efforts seven years after the fact; parents of the slain and injured students were on hand to pay tribute and speak to the crowd. The program began with the speaker announcing, "For all you Marxists... Groucho died today." It defused some of the tension, something needed at the time. But the occasion was serious.

The administration's efforts to end all acknowledgment of May 4 were evident at multiple levels. The university even attempted to "rebrand" as a means to distance itself from May 4. There was even talk about changing the name of the university to the *University of Kent*. A friend who was chairperson of the Greek and Latin Department described this insidious rebranding: "The university president – Schwartz – decided that even the *stationary should be changed*. Kent State University was on the official stationery, but "Kent" was enlarged and bold, and "State" was diminutive. Under pain of administrative reprimand, no professors were permitted to use the old stationary" (Rick Newton, personal communication, December 11, 2022).

In addition, the administration wanted to change the entire "look" and scale of what had formerly been called "Blanket Hill." I remember the area well because I photographed the tents and occupants one foggy morning at the beginning of June. The details were muted, but the colors emerging in the morning were like jewels, with tents of all colors gradually coming into view, albeit muted. It was a beautiful experience, like a "happening" of the 1960s.

But the motivation for subverting the efforts of the activists was far from beautiful. A blatant attempt to distance from its own history, it was considered an insult to activists, students, professors, and families of the injured and slain. It was also an insult to history and remembrance. The entire university was invested in the repression of history. In the process, the controversy surrounding the building of a new gym grew and became entrenched. This was an attempt to move on, away from the events of 1970.

Many in the May 4 community believed that there was plenty of available space on which to build. If one were standing between Taylor Hall and the Pagoda, looking down to the parking lot, the expanse to the right would be obscured by a sprawling construction, the "New Gym." The university had been planning expansions of its physical education facilities into the area that became part of the space where the shootings occurred. This resulted in protests to "Move the Gym," whereby activists set up a Tent City –*Tentropolis* – to keep the bulldozers at bay: "Just as the legal struggles were inconclusive, the gymnasium annex struggle was also inconclusive. The gymnasium annex was built (though it did not

Figure 12.2 "Orphaned" uncredited photograph of the Joan Baez concert and demonstration on the Commons. The author is in the back.

infringe upon the site of the shootings) and an effort to have the site of the shootings declared a National Historic Landmark failed" (Graham, 2006, p. 427).

In hindsight, the activists were correct in their thinking. A decade after construction, the building was becoming obsolete. The location was such that parking was always an issue, and the facilities were inaccessible to students who lived in rentals. It was generally inaccessible to commuters and the community at large. Despite being a sprawling circular building, the facilities were too small. The pool was eventually filled in and the courts were converted into offices and kiosks. A more expansive, practical, and accessible recreation center was built by the newer power plant, located off Summit Street behind campus. Summit Street was remodeled with rotaries and "improved" to facilitate commuter traffic flow. Nearby is the beautiful Presbyterian Church of Kent. A beautiful sanctuary completed in 1969 (nine months before the shootings), paintings and mosaics by Kent State professors adorn the walls. As with Frank Lloyd Wright buildings constructed in solitary, beautiful settings, future development dwarfed and encroached on the site. The sanctuary is currently smothered by multi-tier student housing and a new power plant. The church was envisioned as an abstract sculpture, influenced by the likes of Le Corbusier. It now seems small in comparison to its setting.

110   *The 1970s and My Journey of Understanding*

Figure 12.3 This photo shows Joan Baez singing on the Kent State Commons, August 20, 1977. After some remarks, she has just picked up her guitar to perform. (photograph courtesy of Karl Martin).

Figure 12.4 Activist on the Commons wearing a Richard Nixon mask. His red shirt has lettering that says, "Long live the spirit of Kent and Jackson State. (photo courtesy of Karl Martin).

References

Garrett, A. (July 20, 2005). Kent residence provided killer inspiration. *Daily Kent Stater*.

Graham, M. W. (2006). Memorializing at Kent State University: Reflections on collective memory, public art and religious criticism. *Literature and Theology*, *20*(4), 424–437. http://www.jstor.org/stable/23926968

Hensley, T. R., & Lewis, J. M. (2010). *Kent State and May 4th: A social science perspective*. (Hensley & J. M. (Jerry M. Lewis, Eds.; third edition, revised and expanded.)). Kent State University Press.

Kent State University Library and Archives. *Kent State Tent City: Gym Annex Protest Chronology*.

Ponder, G. A. (1974). The curriculum: Field without a past? *Educational Leadership*, *31*, 461–464.

Radley, Balko (2013). *Rise of the WARRIOR COP: The militarization of America's police forces*. Public Affairs: New York.

13 Representative Patricia Morgan

State Representative Patricia Morgan and I came together in a unique manner. She was roundly criticized for her conservative stance regarding *Critical Race Theory* in a generally "blue" state. As a former Rhode Island resident, I emailed her in a respectful manner, making suggestions as to a less abrasive way to frame her arguments. Patricia is my opposite politically, but we had many commonalities. For example, we shared a fondness for Rhode Island and believed that Kent State University afforded us a good education. Patricia was on campus when the unrest and shootings occurred. She shared her experiences and perspectives about what it was like to be on campus at the time, and we were able to *partially* bridge the political gap. This is what we hope dialogue and discourse engender, leaving the door open to further discussion.

I was reminded of an earlier conversation with children's author Steven Kellogg as we discussed his book *Island of the Skog* and the Pragmatism of John Dewey. I asked him about his motivations for writing a book involving the pursuit of a democratic ideal, and wondered if he might expand:

> I do see where you're going – this was on all our minds in the 60's. When people communicate honestly and forthrightly, they find out that there are more things in common than divide them, and this relates to religious pluralism also. If someone from one faith – or culture – is involved in making an aggressive stance on that rampart they very often eliminate the possibility of working together, learning from each other to work together to solve their problems. It's the only way we can really progress. In the aura of friendship people flourish as individuals.
>
> (Steven Kellogg, personal communication, March 14, 2016)

Patricia: So, what would you like to know? What would you like to talk about?

Karl: I'm guessing you're in a comfortable place?
Patricia: Yes, I'm in my office.
Karl: Please take a few moments to relax, and then we will revisit your experiences on May 4.
Patricia: I was in Altmann Hall, a small honors dormitory. At that time, Kent State was really stunning for a college campus. And there were...what were they called? SDS? Students for a Democratic Society?
K*arl:* Yes.
Patricia: They had burned down the ROTC building on campus, and there was a lot of energy building up around that. It was a time when a lot of students didn't want to go into the military, didn't want to go to war.
(Author's note: It has never been substantiated that the SDS burned the ROTC building.)

And it was kind of a flashpoint. There were protests. We call them protests now, and students gathered down in Kent. I was aware of students gathering down in the town of Kent. They were walking – marching – against the Vietnam War.

Then the SDS burned the ROTC building, and that's when the National Guard showed up to protect other buildings on the campus, and there were troop carriers parked all around. They looked like tanks, but they were troop carriers.

I remember being in some buildings, and they would have National Guardsmen in the buildings. They were young guys, just like us. They were there to make sure that we stayed safe. You were *very aware* of their presence.

At night we had a curfew, and I did have to go off campus once. I went to concert, a violin symphony. I came back after the curfew and there were helicopters flying over campus with spotlights illuminating the ground, to make sure that people were respecting the curfew. It was something you would never expect on an American campus or in the United States.

We had that kind of situation. People were burning down buildings; the National Guard was there with helicopters flying over overhead, and lockdowns. On May 4, the students were going to have a...what do you call it? It was called a *rally*, right? Everybody was going to meet on the Commons at about ten o'clock, something like that. I can't believe I'm still remembering this. This is pretty good.

I was an early riser because I worked in the cafeteria. I was the "cereal girl," pouring the juices and getting cereal out in the morning for people. I got up early every morning, and I had gone to Satterfield Hall for class and then returned to my dorm. Some friends talked about how, you know, we should go to the Commons and see what they're going to say and do.

And I was on my way there when the shooting happened. All of us were ordered back, so I didn't get to the Commons. We were told to go back to our dorm and stay there, and that's what I did. The next day were all told to go home.

That was a tough time for me. My parents had moved away. I didn't know where they were, quite frankly. They were traveling down in Central America somewhere, and by that time might have been in Mexico. There was no way to get in touch with them, so I had no place to go. My sister was two years ahead of me, and we had to search around for jobs. I got a job at Lujan's Big Boy as a waitress, but we didn't have enough money to get our own apartment. We didn't get to go together anywhere. She went with some friends, and I went with some friends, and we spent the summer in separate houses.

And then there was the whole idea of…How do we finish our coursework? Professors got in touch with us, and they put together different kinds of activities and papers that we had to write, and things we had to read. It was a scramble to finish our coursework so that we would get credit for our classes.

And that was my life. It was tough. I was sleeping in a basement and working full time.

14 The Music
Jason Hanley

Vice president of education and visitor engagement at the Rock & Roll Hall of Fame, Jason Hanley earned his PhD in musicology and music history from Stony Brook University in New York. His dissertation was entitled *Metal Machine Music Technology, Noise, and Modernism in Industrial Music from 1975 to 1996*. Recently, we talked about the importance of music surrounding May 4, 1970, at Kent State University.

Jason: Hey, how you doing, Karl?

Karl: I'm fine, and thanks for calling!

Jason: Sorry I didn't get back to you earlier today. It was one of those days where I was busy with stuff, and then I turned around and it was already 4:30.

Karl: Are you in a good place right now? Quiet and comfortable? Relaxed?

Jason: I'm back home now, sitting in a comfy chair, so I'm ready to talk.

Karl: Great! I've been writing about the effects of trauma. It seems like everyone that was on campus on May 4 has residual trauma. According to Dr. Bessel van der Kolk, it surfaces when stress brings those memories back. In your opinion, do you think that music is helpful? Perhaps the music surrounding May 4 embodies the generative power of music?

Jason: I absolutely think that music connects to us directly, with human emotion and memory and the way we think about our memories and deal with them. This is so prevalent that many times people will hear a song, and it immediately brings back a flood of memories to a particular time. And those may be negative or positive memories.

I also think music has the ability – as an art form – to allow people to deal with difficult subjects or difficult situations and process them in a different way. There's just something about the way a musician can write a song that can be based around a traumatic event.

It will allow people to try to process that traumatic event and understand it and maybe connect to it in a different way or look at it in a different light. And I think that's why so many songwriters tend to gravitate towards those sorts of subjects. There are things that we all are thinking or dealing with during times during trauma.

Social upheaval, throughout history, particularly throughout the late 20th century and up to now when rock and roll and popular music have become so important, songwriters will attempt to address what is happening. And you can see that when you look back at themes that musicians have addressed over time.

They often relate to either personal or even global events that – to me – point to a promise of rebirth.

Karl: Yes. I understand, regenerative. ... Were you on the creative team that worked on the May 4 exhibit?

Jason: Yes. I was involved in some of the programming that we did surrounding the remembrances for May 4, and my team with a lot of folks, including people like Craig Werner, who's a great music historian. He has written extensively about particularly Vietnam War songs.

But that also relates directly to Kent State and May 4, the idea of musicians talking about that in relationship to the larger Vietnam story, because of course, music was used frequently, even by American soldiers during the war when they were deployed in Vietnam. And music had a very powerful force, both for the soldiers there but also back home here in the United States for people who had loved ones who were soldiers over in Vietnam, or even just dealing with the social unrest that was happening here in the United States at the time.

Karl: Do any specific songs you consider as emblematic to May 4?

Jason: There's a couple that I always come back to that relate to May 4 and to the Kent State tragedy. The most common and the one most people will probably reference will know and think of immediately is the song "Ohio." It was written by Neil Young, and I think the reason that song continues to stick in so many people's minds is that – as a song – it's an amazing phenomenon.

It happened very quickly after the event, Neil Young wrote the song, and Crosby Stills, Nash and Young, were on the charts at that moment with the song "Teach Your Children." And yeah, I think it was only about two to three weeks after the shootings that they had "Ohio" already pressed as a single and out on the airwaves.

They often told the story of the making of "Ohio." Neil was so moved by the events that he literally just went out and wrote it immediately. They recorded it within a matter of days.

So that's an interesting circumstance where you have an event and a song about that traumatic event that is coming out while people are still processing the event itself. I think for that reason, the song sticks with people so much. Plus, it's an expertly written song. The melody is great.

The rhythm of it captures your attention right away, and the lyrics are very direct. They speak directly to the events of the day, and I think that stays with people. On the other hand, you have examples where famously there are particular lines or references in songs to that moment. For example, John Anderson, the singer of the progressive rock band Yes often talked about a particular line in the song "Long Distance Runaround" that was in reference to the shootings. And the line is, "Hot color melting the anger to stone." That line is not very clear because that's a very interpretive line and could be taken a lot of ways.

...But it's interesting that he felt it was important to add this almost psychedelic interpretation of the moment into the lyric. And then the last thing I always think of isn't a particular song, but the story of the band Devo. And Devo is a really great band from Northeast Ohio, from the Akron area. Many of the original members of the band were students at Kent State at the time.

That includes the Mothersbaugh brothers Mark and Bob. They called their band Devo with the idea that it stood for de-evolution and it was, you know, kind of art rock, verging on New Wave and Industrial Rock, and they thought this was an interesting – almost a joke – concept about how it seemed to them that mankind was beginning to regress. After they experienced the traumatic events of May 4, they decided to stick with that name.

And instead of it being a joke, suddenly Devo became about the real situation that we found ourselves in, and was humanity going to better itself in the long run? Or were we going to devolve into infighting and tearing each other apart? This was addressed in many of their songs throughout their history.

That is an example where the larger concept came directly out of the Kent State massacre, even though it's not a direct reference to any specific song.

All of them had been going to school for other things, and it was at that point when they really decided, "We're gonna do this for real. This is gonna be a real band and we're gonna do this professionally." And they felt very strongly about it. And even to this day, when they create music, they still have that mindset. Devo still uses humorous lyrics, but they use humor and satire to dig at very poignant subjects in American culture.

Karl: How would you encapsulate the role of music in helping with a traumatic experience?

Jason: You know, music connects in a way that a lot of other art forms don't, or a way that writing something down can't. There's some mixture of music and words and rhythm that tap into a part of the human brain that allows us not only to relive something but also process and connect to it. It moves us through something, and we understand it in a new way. And I'll just say that I see that on a regular basis at the Rock & Roll Hall of Fame because it's a unique museum. Many of us love artwork and connect to a Picasso or Van Gogh.

And we love going to an art museum and seeing it on the wall. But the experience that people have at the Rock & Roll Hall of Fame, when they come and they look at, let's say the Beatles exhibit or a Janis Joplin exhibit…they are immediately transported back to moments in their life when they loved that song. Maybe they were sneaking into a concert or traveling across country with their family, listening to the music on a road trip. Or maybe it was a song that was played at a wedding or on a first date with a spouse, or something like that. And we will often see people crying in the exhibits because they're reliving a memory or through the sort of enjoyment of remembering a loved one that passed on or being transported back to an emotional moment.

And the short synopsis of that, even just for my own knowledge, I look at ways that music is seen as political action. I discuss how that music developed as a style and eventually became popular. I consider what happens when a style that's rooted in the avant-garde and political action becomes a style of popular music.

So even from something like coming into a museum, where the artifacts, the music that's playing, and the story we tell in the museum, it connects directly with people. And I think that is really the power of music; the way it lets us come together and connect as humanity.

Karl: Thank you, Jason. Those were wonderful insights.

Jason: I greatly appreciate you asking for my thoughts on the subject, and I'll be honored to read the book when it comes out.

Author's note: At the end of our interview, Jason was notified that David Crosby had passed away. He helped craft the official notice:

Two-time Rock & Roll Hall of Fame Inductee David Crosby was a pioneer of folk-rock and country-rock as a member of the Byrds and Crosby, Stills and Nash, and as a solo artist. Crosby, one of the greatest harmony vocalists of all time, wrote and co-wrote unforgettable songs that expressed the emotional impact of the era, including "Almost Cut My Hair," "Déjà Vu," and "Wooden Ships." He leaves behind a collection and songs that will live on forever.

(Rock & Roll Hall of Fame, January 20, 2023)

15 Final Notes

I have always loved stories. When I was a small child, I used to ask my great uncle – William Henry Sefton – about World War I. He was captured and sent to a prison camp; his stories would eventually become dark. He was lucky because he survived his ordeals. When other adults saw what was happening, I would be yanked away and given verbal reprimands. His memories were riveting. A narrative from Uncle Bill seemed real, and he was a good storyteller. He suffered from post-traumatic stress disorder – called "battle fatigue" – in the Great War, so described because World War II hadn't yet occurred: "Ten million soldiers died and twenty million were wounded in the four years of "the war to end all wars." Those numbers don't include the civilians who died, the children caught in crossfires. At the Battle of Verdun alone, a "battle" that went on for six months, 350,000 Frenchmen and 330,000 Germans died" (Ilyion, 2006, p. 3). Seven hundred and seventy-eight soldiers were killed daily in that war. Uncle Bill returned to Rhode Island after the war and captivity but had trouble pretending nothing had happened. In those days, talking things through was discouraged. Uncle Bill gladly talked with me, and he had my ear. As he shared his memories in language a kid could understand, I learned that war wasn't what we saw in pictures, films, and TV. To me, his conviction and experiences guaranteed authenticity. Uncle Bill could place you *in* the time because he had been *in* the story. I felt the same while listening to the firsthand stories of May 4, 1970. They gave voice to the history, and it has been illuminating. I offer their collected testimonies with some reflections (theirs and mine) and invite the readers to form their own conclusions.

The research has occasionally wandered off into tangential excursions. That is good, because you may discover something you didn't expect, something that can't be scripted. For example, when something terrible happens, something unimaginable, it was Sophie Freud who suggested that we remember *everything* in incredible detail. She spoke from experience. Sophie described riding through France riding bicycles with her mother at night, the sound of Nazi Panzers in the distance. They were displaced from their homeland and pedaling for their very lives. They eventually made their way to the English Channel and awaited boats for escape to England. As she spoke, I could both see *and* hear what she described.

In recollections of Kent State, this phenomenon of memory might be descriptions of puffs of smoke from M1 rifles or screaming in the shooting aftermath. What is recalled to life through remembrance differs among individuals. It is remarkable that vivid details are chiseled into memory, but where does that leave us? Are there essential truths to be found, common denominators of fact in research?

Facts must be uncovered through research, but they should be subject to ongoing analysis. That is an ingredient of Pragmatism, a cyclic circuit of inquiry and review. Self-evident truths are considered nonexistent, only objects of inquiry subject to reevaluation as more information comes to light. Pragmatist scholars Jim Garrison and Mary Leach believe that William James "rejects any notion of a permanent antecedent-fixed essence or identity for researchers to discover. For him there is no perfect end of inquiry, there are only practical purposes" (p. 73).

History may not satisfy our desire to have a convergent solution, but a few new facts and insights may be generated from the work. Historical data and syntheses may need to be reexamined and rewritten to understand our history. As new information comes to light, our nonreflective acceptance and understanding of a historical event may require further work. Some of that may be accomplished through Pragmatist thought, working through habituated beliefs about historical data. Pragmatism originated with Charles S. Peirce (1839–1914), who believed that these habituated beliefs are the mainstay of experience. We think primarily for the limited purpose of getting ourselves out of trouble – that is, when our habits find themselves conflicted or challenged by doubt (Ryan, 2011, p. 21). This is more nonreflective than reflective, and eminently logical, what is called by pragmatists (Ryan) "habituated beliefs." These beliefs as applied to history need revision or not, depending on your politics and theoretical lens. Even so, my guess would be that for pragmatists any theory about all this would have to wait on and follow the particular facts – here personal narratives – rather than what abstractly comes before them.

Kent State made every attempt to disavow its' past. Politicians and pundits blamed "outside agitators" and hippie activists, but over time, new information came to light. It is a tragic and thorny subject, one sure to polarize. One zone guaranteed to generate debate is the ideological underpinning of May 4, 1970, at Kent State. This is our current cultural landscape.

At least nine states have passed laws that make illegal the teaching of "divisive concepts" such as race, sex, or ethnicity. More will likely follow. These issues help us to understand and teach history in a contextual manner, not as absolute or self-evident truths. Consider the history of the Alamo. The history remained unchanged for 150 years: "For the first 150 years after the battle, few disagreed – at least publicly – with the 'traditional' notion that its defenders were fighting for their freedom against the 'oppression' of a crazed Mexican tyrant, Antonio Lopez de Santa Ana. Lots of folks still believe that" (Burrough, Tomlinson & Stanford, 2021, p. 1). History is not fixed; it invites reexamination and rewriting. History may be obscured with misrepresentation and veneer. Even loyal Texans have suggested that the history of the Texas Revolution should be reexamined. Over the course of half a century, the history of May 4, 1970, has been grudgingly reinterpreted.

Nonetheless, political divisions that divided the country during the Vietnam War have remained.

The use of deadly force to quash campus dissent was unwarranted, and we have been lulled into believing that the problem has been resolved, that everything is OK. But things were not well. The students went home, and the campus quieted. This was only a temporary solution because sustained doubt was the result. In other words, despite an unwinding through public opinion and defeat in an unwinnable war, there were unanswered questions from Kent State. Imagine, if you will, being a student in higher education at Kent State. Imagine also military units taking aim at unarmed students, unleashing a hail of bullets for 13 seconds. Consider the depravity, the cruelty, the killing, the screams, and the blood. What must it have been like to visit a dead child at Robinson Memorial Hospital?

Susan Sontag critiques our lack of responsiveness, our lack of feeling: "Someone who is perennially surprised that depravity exists, who continues to feel disillusioned, (even incredulous) when confronted with evidence of what humans are capable of inflicting in the way of gruesome, hands-on cruelties has not reached moral or psychological adulthood" (Sontag, 2003, p. 9). There are many photos from May 4 that illustrate Sontag's passionate treatise, but perhaps none more than the *Kent State Pieta*, with Mary Ann Vecchio and Jeffrey Miller.

The photograph says it all. This is what human beings are capable of. Images like this put an end to superficiality and amnesia. On that note, the curriculum field has not been immune to the amnesia of the present. This kind of superficiality has forsaken the issues of May 4, requiring subsequent generations to rediscover the understanding of their predecessors. This lack of perspective was true for decades at Kent State. There were few studies of a historical nature, and what is continually needed is a dialogue with the past. They might have used, for example, the most psychoanalytic step in currere, the progressive: "The progressive leads not only to what the future can be, but how to get there and what it will look like. As I work toward a synthetical point of view that will impact my choices" (Rose, 2017, p. 40).

As to the role of photography, what truths may be gleaned from a photographic image? What have the photographers included in this writing

Final Notes 123

Figure 15.1 Mary Ann Vecchio screams as she kneels over the body of Kent State University student Jeffrey Miller (1950–1970), shot during the anti-war demonstration on the university campus, Kent, Ohio, May 4, 1970. Photo courtesy of John Filo, Getty Images, and the Kent State Library and Archives.

wrought from behind the viewfinder? Beaumont Newhall – photographer and historian – included the writing of Albert Sands Southworth (1871) to illuminate: "But the artist, even in photography, must go beyond discovery and knowledge of facts. He must create and invent truths and produce new development of facts. (…) …he should be informed as to the principles which govern or influence human actions, and the causes which affect and mark human character" (Newhall, 1980, p. 41).

Consider the iconic photograph John Darnell took at the exact moment the National Guard turned and fired. Is not a photographic representation more than light and shadow? Even for persons unfamiliar with the history, it's impossible to take your eyes away from it. The moment in time is arrested, clear and sharp, the composition flawless. It is almost *too perfect*, like the staged recreation of the raising of the flag at Iwo Jima. General Canterbury is entering the frame, gas mask raised as he orders the shooting to stop. Dressed in a suit, he *must* take another step. He *must* shout a command that stops the carnage. At the other side of the image is Sergeant Myron Pryor, crouching as he extends his left hand and .45 caliber pistol. In between are the members of Company G that *must* secure a target, *must* press the triggers of their M1 rifles. The photograph can't reveal their expressions, an anonymity afforded by the gas masks, but the viewer is given a lot of information. It seems perfectly composed, yet we know the landscape continues past the photo. The image is rich and detailed yet sweeping in meaning as it reconstructs the past. You can see it plainly. Their hands grip the rifles. There is something relaxed in their positions, some primal, gracefully terrible. Framed by the fence and the Pagoda, Darnell has captured so much information into one frame.

Some have given themselves to the killing, Myron Pryor taking away his body as a target as he turns sideways in his crouch. The others are purposeful in their posture, in their attitude. They seem deliberate, focused, and unhurried. Since they were at the summit, the only problem might have been shooting downward, down the hill. This may have not been a large issue because the M1 uses a single peep aperture that accommodates elevation. The adjustment apparatus relies on "clicks." Each "click" you feel and hear as you turn the elevation pinion changes the strike of the bullet. One *MOA* (minutes of angle) means it is one inch up or down at 100 yards, two inches at 200 yards, and so on. This would be second nature to experienced marksmen. The guardsmen who intended to shoot individual students only had to keep the fingers of the right hand relaxed, and the left arm unmoving. A small adjustment could make a person come into the peep sight. If the shot was lined up correctly, she or he was hit.

Figure 15.2 Company G ascended the hill, turned, and fired in unison (photograph courtesy of John Darnell). He personally sent this image to me, and the clarity is phenomenal.

Darnell has exquisitely captured a terrible moment, the second as lives were lost. We believe that the past is gone, that the future hasn't yet happened, and only the present exists. This photograph deconstructs that misconception. And the image was nearly lost. I asked him about his process, how he was able to focus through the viewfinder under duress:

> It wasn't about keeping my composure, but about taking the photos, then keeping them away from National Guardsmen who tried to seize my negatives. (I gave them a couple of blank roles I had in my pocket!). Seeing the bodies on the ground, I felt extreme grief and sadness.
>
> (John Darnell, personal communication, January 11, 2023)

May 4 is a fascinating topic. It exposes dark elements in the America of 1970 and today. Any perspectives and syntheses are secondary to the stories of the participants. I believed that a book with "currere" in the title needed this narrative. Something very special here that deserved to see the light of day. This writing offers, at best, disquiet. At the center is a compelling story that may help people understand new avenues of currere thought. It's not exclusively about the method, pared down and focused. It's not simply about May 4 either. It is a journey through the educational experiences of people who were there. In the end, I wanted to share their stories and what they teach us about learning, living, and being.

These events clearly shaped the paths of their lives. Trained in a variety of disciplines, all have eventually woven education into their missions and vocations. Each one has used an informal method of currere to "make sense" of things and generate some sort of hope or call to action for future generations. For practical purposes, we may call this "making things of sense."

Recently, Kent State had a showing of *Fire in the Heartland* followed by a discussion with panelists involved in anti-Vietnam demonstrations 52 years ago. It was suggested that students should become politically active because of the current political climate. Since the spirit of Kent State arises every May 4, it may as well grow and flourish here. Is there growing fascism in the country's current political climate? Madeleine Albright's new book suggests believes that fascist governments of the 1930s and 1940s have laid the groundwork for today: "[A] fascist is someone who identifies strongly with the claims to speak for a whole nation or group, is unconcerned about the rights of others and is willing to use whatever means are necessary – including violence – to achieve his or her goals" (p. 11). A friend and colleague recently penned the following ominous reflections:

> The main May 4th speaker was Jon Meacham, a Pulitzer Prize winning presidential biographer. His highly reflective comments about the May 4th tragedy were, in many respects, a warning about how democracy had failed us on that day. He said that "those in power declared war on

the people." The National Guard troops that murdered and wounded 13 students peacefully demonstrating against the Vietnam War were not convicted of their killings. Neither was Ohio's governor, James Rhodes charged with ordering the Guard to campus to control the students. So, the government was blameless. Meacham said, "May 4th is recognized as one of the bloodiest college/university events in American history" Wilen, W. (2022) AIJR.

Sometime between 1972 and 1973, art students from Kent State and Akron formed a band called Devo, the namesake of the social theory of de-evolution. The shootings pushed them into satire and social commentary through music. I still own a button from one of their concerts, an image of a chicken with a man's head. In an interview with *Rolling Stone*, Devo bassist and former art student Jerry Casale talked about the sour relationship between the university and the conservative townspeople and Ohio governor Jim Rhodes fanning the flames. Jerry encapsulated the aftermath when he said,

> [S]tudent organized protest was over. Nobody was gathered. You kill a few students and that really works. The activists left town or went into hiding or joined the Weather Underground. Other kids cut their hair and went to work for their dads, who had been bugging them to get it together. Kent State killed the movement.
>
> (Greene, 2020, para 40)

Leaders possessing fascist beliefs and behaviors exist both in the United States and throughout the world. Missing in their agendas and platforms are history, knowledge, and rational thinking. Current political issues are also educational issues. The shootings of students on their own campus by the forces of law and order describe a withered culture still evidenced today: "At a time when social justice is under enormous attack, when the right wing dominates a whole range of cultural apparatuses, education becomes vital. And it must be defined through the claims that it makes on democracy" (Henry Giroux).

Authoritarianism rejects any form of critical pedagogy. This has engendered a helplessness in society and culture based on authoritarianism and the sovereignty of the state. Since May 4, it may have taken on a different form, but it's still there. The student activists had political agency, but it was repressed. It reemerged at Kent State in the spring and summer of 1977. Over time, an individualistic culture has emerged, a culture that eschews all manner of historical consciousness. New generations are left to rediscover the history and historical knowledge. Questions of historical consciousness are rendered inert. It seems that history no longer really matters unless it's a contrived authoritarian history that smacks of management.

This trend toward ahistoricism is not a new phenomenon. Social responsibility is integral to what we label as "historical memory." Education is vital to a democracy, and this writing hopes to contribute to the education and civic consciousness that accompanies the narratives of May 4. In an ordinary town like Kent, Ohio, something terrible and extraordinary happened. As a result, ordinary people became extraordinary in their work, dedicated to keeping the memory of May 4 alive. This writing is dedicated to acknowledging their work and vision.

Wandering across the commons and the site of the shootings can be an ordinary endeavor. One must get to a class, the student center, or an office. When pausing to reflect, it's easy to remember or understand the enormity of what happened. Concerned individuals have made certain that history hasn't gone away and tried to guard against reinterpretations and denials. Their memories are vital to something larger, a historical memory. They didn't want Kent State and May 4 to become an afterthought in history books.

Alistair Begg, a well-known pastor and radio personality from Cleveland has attempted to describe the worrisome lack of persistence in memory: "And not many of us, if any of us, will even be a footnote in history books. Our great grandchildren may not even be able to spell our first name. They may never even know anything about us at all. Forget our great-grandchildren – our grandchildren themselves" (Alistair Begg, 2001, *God of the Ordinary*). Revisiting the past keeps the memory of societal issues at the forefront.

Long after the disregard for human life and lack of integrity fades from memory, writing will give an accounting of what happened, and why it happened. As applied to the history of the Kent State shootings, the testimonies may be seen on a larger stage as allegory. Incorporating the public world requires the use of allegory, "evident in the new curriculum metaphor of allegory which means to 'speak publicly at an assembly'" (Doll, 2017, p. 173). The history revisited in this writing, Pinar's (2012) inclusion of "allegory" in his multiple "curriculum-as-*currere*" explications, incorporates the past into the present: "Historical facts are primary, but it is their capacity to invoke our imagination that marks them as allegorical. Their meanings are not confined to the past; they leak into our experience of the present" (Pinar, 2015, p. 28). It is my hope that this will introduce – or reintroduce – the tragedy of May 4, 1970, to a larger audience.

The Latin phrase "Verba Volant Scripta Manent" is translated as "Spoken words fly away, written words remain." It inspires me to share these testimonies in writing. I trust that history isn't forgotten or misinterpreted, thanks to the enduring value of the written word.

A few days before he died, George Harrison said, "You know, all of our past is gone. And the future we don't know anything about. All that we have is now." He was speaking existentially, focusing on the present through a Buddhist temporal perspective. History *does* exist; it isn't gone, and it is relevant. Historians do important work, from field research to getting it down in writing. This is the allegorical component of currere, expansion into a public world. History is still here; it's back behind the curve in the road. We can recreate – reactivate – the events by stopping the car, getting out, and retracing our route.

As I look back on how this began, some of the value of the inquiry lies in the questions that it raises and the cross-fertilization of experiences and ideas that it engendered. I've tried to include more of the interview transcripts than is necessary in order to show the interviewees as real human beings. Perhaps we've looked at things a little differently as we met one another for the first time and will continue to search for accurate synopses that safeguard and preserve the heritage. Meanwhile, we examine what has been said and written in the past (which regularly accumulates), and how to make the history available to a larger audience.

Synthesis and Conclusion: A Call to Action

The greatest insights are often subtle, nuggets of wisdom that need to be revisited to gain momentum. The persons I've spoken with have been the embodiment of grace, generosity, and kindness. They met with me in trust, faith, and a shared interest in the pursuit of peace and justice. I'm better for having known them. The profound knowledge I've distilled from this journey has been overwhelming, and I'm grateful to be able to share their stories as currere reexaminations of their experiences. Through their testimony, common threads emerge, beginning with an admonition against using excessive force to quash political dissent. In that light, the lessons of May 4, 1970, are still relevant today, perhaps more than ever. The interview testimonies represent "difficult returns" to the events of May 4, and it is hoped that people and events keep their place and legacy in history. The violence of May 4 renders an unstable finality but will serve to help us "live with what cannot be redeemed, what must remain a psychic and social wound that bleeds" (Simon, Rosenberg, and Eppert, 2000, p. ix). I am hopeful for a future that is bettered from working through this traumatic event.

There is always more to see and hear, and I look forward to new perspectives and new knowledge. I am hopeful that currere narratives surrounding the tragedy of May 4, 1970, will inform a collective journey of understanding, something bettered from working through this traumatic catastrophe. Firsthand experiences of eyewitnesses help to make sense of May 4, 1970, and the educational world.

Figure 15.3 Blanket Hill, Don Drumm's *Solar Totem* and the Pagoda, 2021. photograph courtesy of the author).

The narratives have parallels that are still topical. Without keeping history alive and at the forefront, another strongman mayor, governor, police unit, or military branch of the government may arise and suppress. We've witnessed the increased militarization of police and political figures intending to subvert democracy as we know it. This is not an abstract fear. It may – and has – emerge as real, dangerous, and deadly. And it runs deeper. Theorist and scholar Henry Giroux believes that systematic violence is part of a neoliberal, punishing state: "The neoliberal killing machine is on the march globally. The spectacle of neoliberal misery is too great to deny any more and the only mode of control left by corporate-controlled societies is violence, but a violence that is waged against the most disposable such as immigrant children, protesting youth, the unemployed, the new precariat and black youth" (Giroux, H. *Truthout*, 2020). Civil liberties must not be dismantled.

Giroux presents a bleak picture of systematic violence culturally inherent then and now. He presents the other side of modernism's face, with threats to the status quo systematically and ruthlessly quashed. Barbarism was evident during the late 1960s and on May 4, with reform movements and ideas countermanded by agencies of the state. It seemed dystopian and unjust. I reached out to Professor Gregory Claeys of the Royal Holloway University of London, an expert on modern social and political thought. He remembered the events well, as he started college a few months later and became of draft age the following year:

> Many societies have become so much more dystopian since then that four deaths seem paltry by comparison to the likely fate of hundreds of millions as the environment collapses. One basic message, though, is that the theme of dystopia-as-dictatorship, central to the literary tradition since the late 19th century, involves the militarization of politics, and now, of police forces in notionally liberal democracies. The National Guard should not have been called out at Kent State – you'll remember the violence at Chicago in 1968, but there were no shootings there as I recall. The message today seen from Britain, where the right to protest has been severely curtailed in the past year, is to protect that right to the maximum extent. For we have many more protests to come and the shift towards authoritarianism in many countries has become a very alarming trend.
>
> (Gregory Claeys, personal communication, November 13, 2022)

It seems like there can't be an easy synthesis in this history, something to hold onto as truth. I offer testimonies to read and consider. Please keep in mind that this violent response occurred at a public university, a public educational institution. Students were wounded physically and psychologically, having to overcome hardships for decades. Despite this, all have attempted to live expressive and creative lives. Coming together annually to reflect with other survivors and interested persons, the May 4 community doesn't always present a united front. After all, they are activists, philosophers, poets, and even teachers. They have commonalities because agents of state authority sundered their lives. It was part of a larger problem, rooted in what most thought was an unjust war. Societal control prevailed through a totalitarianism veiled as law and order.

Each has vivid memories they are willing to share, and I believe they are accurate, if not slightly reconfigured. Tom Poetter of Miami University describes two sides of the memory dialectic. He doesn't remember details from decades past without linking them to experiences, emotions, or traumatic events:

> It is the case, though, that my memories of my school days have remained vivid. I also realize that these memories are constantly reconfigured as I age, and as time passes, there is no doubt that they have become much less rigorously accurate and, I daresay, at least to a degree, fictionalized.
>
> (Poetter, 2022, p. 3)

A song written by Justin Hayward of the Moody Blues was released in April of 1970 immediately before this piece of history. It was entitled "Question" and described the prevailing angst of that time. Their governing questions have grown even more pressing in the past decades.

Why do we never get an answer
When we're knocking at the door
With a thousand million questions
About hate and death and war?

References

Burrough, B., Tomlinson, C., & Stanford, J. (2021). *Forget the Alamo: The rise and fall of an American myth*. Penguin Press: New York.

Newhall, B., Ed. (1980). *Photography: Essays and images: Illustrated readings in the history of photography*. The Museum of Modern Art. New York: New York Graphic Society: Boston.

Rose, B. (2017). Progressing into *currere*'s progressive: Taking action for an unknown future. *Currere Exchange Journal, 1*(1), 40–48.

Ryan, F. X. (2011). Seeing together: Mind, matter and the experimental outlook of John Dewey and Arthur F. Bentley. *Economic Bulletin, 51,* (11).

Sontag, S. (2003). Photography. Media Foundations.

Index

Pages in *italics* refer to figures.

Achilles 20–21
The Aeneid 12
Agamemnon 20
Agnew, Spiro T. 11, 18, 90
The Agora in Cleveland 83
Akron Boulevard 43, 47
Akron University 91–92
Albright, Madeleine 125
Alliance 91
Altmann Hall 113
antiwar activism 2
anti-war movement 84, 92, 102
architecture building 60
Arendt, H. 26
audiophiles 61
authoritarianism 126
autobiography 31, 47

Baez, Joan 28, *29*, 108–109, *109–110*
band Devo 117–118, 126
bayonets 6–7, 59–60, 86
BB rifle 47
Beacon Journal 47
Beaton, Lynn Csernotta 56–63
Begg, Alistair 22, 127
Blanket Hill 7, 54, 59, 62, 73, 103, 106, 108, *129*
Bloch, Robert 106
"blue-collar" Democrats 97
The Body Keeps the Score 66, 93
Boston Psychiatric Society and Institute 36

Cadwell, Kathy 35
Cambodia 1–2, 5–6, 11, 53
campus 15, 79–80, 82, 87, 113, 122

Canfora, Alan 7, 49–55, *53*, 56, 58
Canton 84, 88–89
Casale, Jerry 126
"Chic" Canfora, Roseann 23, 99–104
Claeys, Gregory 129
Clark University 32
Cleary, John 7, 55, 71–81, *72*, 87, 90
Cleveland 64–65, 68, 127
Cleveland Federal Court in 1975 54
Cole, Sarah 12
collaborative lead-learning 51
Columbia University 14
The Commons 11, 44, 59, 73, 79, 84, 103, 106–107, *110*, 114
Company G members 27, 123, *124*
Concerned Citizens Community of Kent 84
Congress 6
consonance 99
cover of *Life* magazine 76, 78, 87, 89
COVID-19 pandemic 53
Critical Race Theory 112
Cronkite, Walter 1
Crosby, David 11, 116, 119
Cullum, Joe 7, 78, 82–96
Currere, four-step process 4, 14, 77
curriculum 15, 18, 21–26, 38–39
The Curriculum 13
"curriculum-as-*currere*" 127
Cuyahoga River 9

Daley, Richard J. 23
Darnell, John *50*, 123–125
Dean Kahler 101
Dean Kaylor 54
Democratic National Convention 102

Department of Education 2
Dewey, J. 15, 19, 61, 100, 104–105
Dickey, James 102
dissonance 99
Doll Jr., William 13
Dorgan, Margaret 33
draft card 2, *2*
draft eligibility 2
Drumm, Don 25, *25*, 103, 106, *129*
Duffy, Norm 44

Eight-Year Study 13
Eisner, E. 56
Elgin House 106
Ellison, Harlan 83
Ellsberg, Daniel 3
Engleman Hall 11
eyewitness testimony 95–96

FedEx 66
Ferenczi, Sandor 35
Filo, John 16, 24, 100
Fire in the Heartland 125
Five Lectures on Psychoanalysis 35
Florence Heller School of Social Welfare 31
The Fountainhead and *Atlas Shrugged* 12
France 61, 120
Frank, Glenn 3, 41, 46, 72, 88
Freedom of Information Act 79
Freire, P. 17
Freud, Anna 37
Freud, Sigmund 31–32, 35–36, 39
Freud, Sophie 31–39, 120
Friday night 6, 64, 73
Friedlander, S. 81

Garrison, Jim 121
Gary Minerva 83
General Canterbury 6–7, 11, 18, 123
Giroux, Henry 129
Gless, Patricia 41–42
Golding, Brage 103–104
Gordon, William 93
Grace, Tom 55
The Greeks 19–21
Gregory, S. W. 28
Grimm, Nancy 106
Grumet, Madeleine 13, 17
guardsmen 7, 43–45, 78–79; decisions by 47; deployed on campus adjacent *48*; fired 55; in traffic on Main Street *103*; use bayonets and tear gas 6
Guernica 16
Guided Currere Narrative 4
guided regression 17
gunshots 65

Hanley, Jason 115–119
Harrison, George 127
Hassler, David 68
Hayward, Justin 131
Heller School 31
Henderson, James G. 15
Hendry, Petra 18–19
heroic wanderers 12
historical memory 127
House Bill 6, 90
Huebner, D. E. 13–14, 17, 33

"II-S" deferments 1
The Iliad 99
informal *currere* exploration 57
Island of the Skog 112

James J. Jackson Putnam Children's Center 31–32, 35–36
James, William 32, 121
Jawbone 68
Johnson, Robert 3, 55
Jones, Harry 47
Joyce, Nancy Csernotta 64–70
Jung, Carl 35

Keller, Helen 37
Kellogg, Steven 112
Kent City Police Station 107
Kent City Schools 2, 83, 102
Kent Historical Society 106
Kent on Friday night 64
Kent State 76, 82; 1970 shootings *see* May 4, 1970; protest 54; tour by Alan Canfora 53–55, 58; tragedy 116
Kent State Pieta 16
Kent State University 1–4, 52; cops 44; shootings at *see* shootings at Kent State; students killed and wounded at *see* May 4, 1970
Kent State University Board of Trustees 106–107
Kitner, Harold 105
Kiwanis Club presentation 91
Kliebard, Herbert 13

Index

Kolb, Van Der 37
Krause, Allison 7, 46, 48, 54

Laffey, M. 27
law enforcement authorities 87
Leach, Mary 121
The Lester Lefton Esplanade 80
Lewis, J. M. 16, 28, 43–48, *44*, 67, 93, 105
Lewis, Joe 7, 55, 74, 87
Life Magazine on May 6, 1970 71
Lofgren, Nils 83
Longcoy School Olympics of 1976 43
"Long Distance Runaround" song 117
Louisville 1
Lowers, Jennifer 51
The Lure of the Transcendent 17
Lynn 64, 66–68

M1 bullet hole 25, *25*
M1 rifles 121, 123–124
MacDonald, James B. 14
Main Street 86, 88
Martin, K. 43–55; interview with experiences of May 4, 1970 *see* May 4, 1970; motivation 35, 76; and Sophie Freud *33*, 33–35; at Victory Bell, Winter 1978 *107*
Martin Luther King 23
Massachusetts 82
May 3, 1970 *10*, 62
May 4, 1970 9, 12, 15, 18–19, 49, 125; commemorations 26, 71; events of 19, 48, 56, 72, 128; history of 121–122; Jason Hanley 115–119; Joe Cullum 82–96; John Cleary 72–81; Lynn Csernotta Beaton 58–61; Nancy Csernotta Joyce 64–70; Patricia Morgan 112–114; people ducking and running *41*; Roseann "Chic" Canfora 97–104; site 107, 109, 127; survivors of 19, 101; tragedy 21, 52, 125, 128
May 4 memorial by John Cleary *80*
May 4 Presidential Advisory Committee 22
May 4 symposiums 77
May 4 Task Force 22, 75, 103, 107
McGilvrey Hall *95*
McNamara, Robert S. 16
McNees, Ronald P. *78*
Meacham, Jon 125

memor(y/ies) 18, 42, 62, 67, 71–72, 76–77, 94–95, 130
memorializing 26–27
method of *currere* 3–7, 13–14, 32, 36–37, 76
Michener, James 93, 106
military service 2, 89
Miller, Greg 92
Miller, Jeff 54, 90–92
Miller, Jeffrey *24*, 48, 122, *123*
minutes of angle (MOA) 124
modernism 11–13, 129
modernist individualism 12
Moody Blues 131
Morgan, Patricia 112–114
Move the Gym controversy of 1977–1978 27, *29*, 52, 108
music 115–119

Nash, Graham 11, 116, 119
National Guard/Guardsmen 15, 18, 28, 43, 49, 58, 64, 86–87, 125, 130; in buildings 113; commons toward pagoda *50*; fired 46; helicopters flying over 113; jeep 11; on Lincoln Street *95*; personnel walking toward crowd *4*; in town and on campus *85*; troops 59, 126
National Institute of Education (NIE) 13
Nazi Brown Shirts 89–90
Nazi Panzers 120
Nazi Party militia 90
New Deal Democrat 89
Newhall, B. 123
"newly espoused myths" 97–99
Newton, Rick 19–20
The New Yorker magazine 31
New York Times 18
Nimoy, Leonard 105
Nixon, Richard 2–3, 5, 9, 11–13, 26, 53–54, 89–90, 94, 101
North Water Street 6
November 4, 2021 58–63

Ohio history 67–68
Ohio National Guard 6–7, 27; *see also* National Guard/Guardsmen
Ohio State 82
Olds, Glenn 107

Pagoda 45, 73–74, 99, 108, 124
The Pagoda 25

Partially Buried Woodshed 106
Peirce, Charles S. 121
Pemetti, Guy 106
Pentagon papers 16
Perkins Pancake House 66
photography 122–124, *123*
Pinar, W. F. 4, 11, 13, 17, 33, 38–39, 51
Pittsburgh 75, 88
poetry books 69–70
Poetter, Tom 130
political ideologies 14
popular music 118
post-modernism 13
poststructuralism 18
pragmatism 63, 112, 121
Prentice Gate *98*
Prentice Hall 7, 26, 45–46, 60
protestors 3, 73, 84, 93
Pryor, Myron 45, 123–124
Psycho House 106
public memory 26
public universities 97, 130

Radcliffe College of Harvard University 31
Ragain, Maj 68–70
Rand, Ayn 12
Rashomon 95
Ravenna 88–89
realm of currere 81
reconceptualization 57
regressive phase of *currere* 3
repression 42, 52, 108
Republican party 90
reunions 77
Rhode Island 112, 120
Rhodes, James 6, 9, 11, 23, 89
Rhodes, Jim 126
Roazen, P. 36
Robinson Memorial Hospital 41–42, 68, 71, 122
Rock & Roll Hall of Fame 115, 118–119
ROTC building 26, 44, 64, 85, 94, 98, 113
Royal Holloway University of London 129
Ruffner, Howard 76, 78–79, 87
Russell Hall 1
Ryan, F. X. 19

Sappho 18
Satrom, LeRoy 3, 6, 9, 11

Satterfield Hall 113
Scheuer, Sandra 45, 48
School of Media and Journalism 99
Schroeder, William 48
Schwartz 28
Scranton Commission 7, 18, 46
Selective Service Registration 2
Shock, William 105
shootings at Kent State 1–7, 10–11, 16, 18, 23, 25, 28, 43–44, 49, 52, 56–58, 60, 63, 68, 84, 98, 101, 106, 108–109, 117, 127
Silent Sam 26
Silver Oaks 59, 65–66, 93
Simmons School of Social Work 31
Simon, Roger 37
Smithson, Robert 106
Solar Totem 25, *25*, 103, 106, *129*
song "Ohio" 116–117
Sontag, S. 122
sound of gunfire 62
Southworth, Albert Sands 123
sovereignty of the state 126
Stark County 82
Stills, Stephen 11, 116, 119
Stony Brook University 115
The Story of My Life 37
Students for a Democratic Society (SDS) 84, 106, 113
Sullivan, Anne 37
Summit Street 90, 109
Supreme Court 1

Taylor Hall 3, *4*, 7, 10–11, 22, 44, 49, 52, 73–74, 86, 106, 108
"Teach Your Children" song 116
Tentropolis 108
Three Brothers 37
Three Identical Strangers 37
Todd, Diacon 22
totalitarianism 130
trauma 12, 20–21, 38–39, 52, 66, 71, 77, 81, 93, 115
traumatic events 116–117, 128, 130
Tri Towers 93
Troop G 7, 54–55
Tucker, E. Bruce 35
Twain, Mark 23
Tyler, Ralph 13, 51
Tyler Rationale 13

Uncle Bill 120
United States 6, 12, 16–17, 31, 39, 113

van der Kolk, Bessel 93, 115
Vecchio, Mary Ann 24, *24*, 122, *123*
"Verba Volant Scripta Manent" 127
Victory Bell 11, 86
Vietnam 6, 84, 91–92
Vietnamization 2
Vietnam War 1, 3, 16, 23, 101, 122
violence 12, 16, 23

Walden Pond 33, 35
Warren, Beverly 22, 102
Water Street 9
Weldes, J. 27

Werner, Craig 116
Westminster College 1, 3
White House 3
White, Robert I. 3, 9
Wick Poetry Center 68–69
World War I 12, 120
World War II 120
wounded students 41–42, 45–46, 75, 103, 107
Wright, Frank Lloyd 109

Yale University 55, 63
Young, Neil 11, 116–117
Youngstown 88

For Product Safety Concerns and Information please contact our EU
representative GPSR@taylorandfrancis.com
Taylor & Francis Verlag GmbH, Kaufingerstraße 24, 80331 München, Germany